# VEGAS '69

## The Story of The King's Return to the Concert Stage

## Ken Sharp

JETFIGHTER

# ELVIS
## VEGAS '69

# CAST

**elvis presley**

**paul anka**

**steve binder**
director, *Singer Presents Elvis*

**bruce banke**
assistant director
of publicity and advertising,
International Hotel

**rona barrett**
gossip columnist

**chris bearde**
co-writer,
*Singer Presents Elvis*

**bill belew**
Elvis's costume designer

**terry blackwood**
The Imperials

**rodney bingenheimer**
music writer, *Go* magazine

**pat boone**

**myram borders**
writer, *Nevada State Journal*

**estelle brown**
The Sweet Inspirations

**lindsey buckingham**
Fleetwood Mac

**james burton**
lead guitar, TCB Band

**glen campbell**

**richard carpenter**
The Carpenters

**carol channing**

**dave clark**
The Dave Clark Five

**petula clark**

**maria columbus**
concert attendee

**ray connolly**
music writer,
*London Evening Standard*

**cricket mendell coulter**
fan

**david dalton**
music writer,
*Rolling Stone*

**roger daltrey**
The Who

**mac davis**
songwriter, "In The Ghetto"

**jackie deshannon**

**fats domino**

**joe esposito**
Memphis Mafia

**don felder**
The Eagles

**phil everly**
The Everly Brothers

**lamar fike**
Memphis Mafia

**bob finkel**
executive producer,
*Singer Presents Elvis*

**john fogerty**

**d.j. fontana**
drums

**ace frehley**
KISS

**jean-marc gargiulo**
concert attendee

**shecky greene**
comedian

**gloria greer**
ABC-TV local reporter

**george hamilton**

**glen d. hardin**
piano, TCB Band

**dusty hill**
ZZ Top

**cissy houston**
The Sweet Inspirations

**bones howe**
music director,
*Singer Presents Elvis*

**chris hutchins**
European press representative
for International Hotel/creative
director, Tom Jones

**chris isaak**

**mike jahn**
music writer, *New York Times*

**mark james**
songwriter, "Suspicious Minds"

**felton jarvis**
Elvis's producer

**tom jones**

**bill jost**
assistant maître d',
International Hotel Showroom

**june juanico**
former girlfriend

**carol kaye**
concert attendee

**kirk kerkorian**
owner, International Hotel

**joseph kereta**
elvisnow.com

**andy klein**
concert attendee

**GEORGE KLEIN**
Memphis Mafia

**millie kirkham**
background soprano vocalist

**MARTY LACKER**
Memphis Mafia

**LANCE LEGAULT**
Elvis's friend and movie
stunt double

**FRANK LIEBERMAN**
*Los Angeles Herald-Examiner*

**bill medley**
The Righteous Brothers

**bill miller**
talent booker,
International Hotel

**sandi miller**
fan

**ARMOND MORALES**
The Imperials

**richard moreno**
security, International Hotel,
1969-1973

**bobby morris**
orchestra leader,
Bobby Morris Orchestra

**joe moscheo**
The Imperials

**ANN MOSES**
editor, *Tiger Beat* magazine/
Hollywood correspondent
for *New Musical Express*

**LARRY MUHOBERAC**
piano, TCB Band

**emilio muscelli**
head showroom maître d',
International Hotel, 1969-1977

**SCOTTY MOORE**
guitar

**jimmy mulidore**
Joe Guercio Orchestra

**nicholas naff**
director of Advertising and
Publicity, International Hotel

**jimmy newman**
executive vice-president
of Casino Operations,
International Hotel

**colonel tom parker**

**loanne miller parker**
secretary for Alex
Shoofey, president of the
International Hotel and
Colonel Parker's Widow

**patti parry**
Elvis's personal friend

**joe perry**
Aerosmith

**lisa marie presley**

**priscilla presley**

**johnny rivers**

**paul rodgers**
Bad Company

**tom sarnoff**
NBC west coast
vice-president of Production
and Business Affairs

**jerry scheff**
bass, TCB Band

**jerry schilling**
Memphis Mafia

**t.g. sheppard**
then known as
**bill browder**,
head of Southeast Regional
Promotion, RCA Records

**Alex shoofey**
president, International Hotel

**sammy shore**
comedian

**don short**
music writer, *The Daily Mirror*

**paul simon**

**NANCY SINATRA**

**myrna smith**
The Sweet Inspirations

**david stanley**
Elvis's step-brother

**paul stanley**
KISS

**RINGO STARR**
The Beatles

**gordon stoker**
The Jordanaires

**ian fraser-thomson**
concert attendee

**lou toomin**
Alex Shoofey's personal friend

**pete townshend**
The Who

**RONNIE TUTT**
drummer, TCB Band

**bobby vinton**

**RAY WALKER**
The Jordanaires

**mike weatherford**
author, *Cult Vegas*

**SONNY WEST**
Memphis Mafia

**john wilkinson**
rhythm guitar, TCB Band

# iNTRODUCTiON

Las Vegas is a one-stop destination of hedonism and heartbreak, a bacchanalian playground of excess where dreams are made, and just as quickly shattered.

"Bright light city gonna set my soul, gonna set my soul on fire, got a whole lot of money that's ready to burn so get those stakes up higher…" sang Elvis on the Doc Pomus and Mort Shuman penned classic, "Viva Las Vegas," a song which vividly extolled the allure of Sin City, a town redolent in images of flashing neon signs, beautiful women, and non-stop 24-hour action, all predicated on that one lucky roll of the dice, a winning blackjack hand or slot machine jackpot. Today Elvis and Las Vegas are synonymous, joined at the hip, iconic touchstones in popular culture.

But back in 1956, after a disastrous two-week engagement at Las Vegas's New Frontier Hotel, no one could have predicted that Elvis Presley, whose performance was trashed by the *Las Vegas Sun* newspaper as "a bore" and *Newsweek* who noted that the audience "sat through Presley as if he were a clinical experiment," would turn the town upside down a mere thirteen years later.

There's an old adage that says you can't go home again but sometimes that just isn't true. After a protracted eight year absence from live performances, Elvis Presley was able to find his way home again and his path would lead him directly to the concert stage. Reinvigorated by the tremendous critical and commercial success of the *Singer Presents Elvis* TV special and soon to be enjoying his first number one hit in seven years, "Suspicious Minds," on July 31, 1969, Elvis took to the stage at the International Hotel in Las Vegas with something to prove. Inside the 2,000 seat showroom, packed with celebrities, VIP's and high rollers, Elvis delivered the show of a lifetime, proving to all in attendance that he was clearly back where he belonged and poised to carve out an exciting new chapter in his illustrious career.

*Elvis: Vegas '69* tells the remarkable story of Elvis Presley's triumphant return to the concert stage, as told through first-hand accounts by those lucky enough to be on hand to witness the King's miraculous artistic and creative rebirth.

But before we jump ahead, let's rewind back to the year 1968 where we find a lost Elvis, stuck in a deepening quagmire of creative disappointment and career stagnation.

INTERNATIONAL
HOTEL
LAS VEGAS, NEVADA

PRESENTS

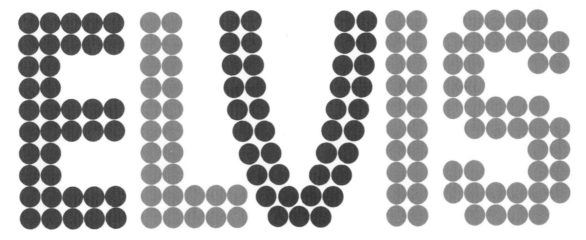

ELVIS

AUGUST **1969** AUGUST

IN

# PERSON

# hollywood heartbreak

By the late '60s, Elvis's career was on life support. He was stuck in a soulless rut, forced to endure an endless treadmill of formula laden movies, none of which captured the acting promise Elvis displayed in such seminal films as *Jailhouse Rock* and *King Creole*. Seemingly relegated to being a prop in his own films, his frustration increased due to the lousy scripts and inane songs like "Old MacDonald," "Yoga is as Yoga does," and "Dominic," a song about a bull. If his career were to survive, something had to change. ...and quick.

**elvis presley:** It was work. It was a job. I had to be there at a certain time of the morning and work a certain amount of hours and that's exactly how I treated it. I was more concerned if the picture was any good or I was any good. I cared so much until I became physically ill. I would become violently ill. I'd get a temperature. At a certain stage I had no say so in the script so I couldn't say this was not good for me. I didn't have final approval of the script, which means that I couldn't say this was not good for me. I don't think anyone was consciously trying to harm me. It was just Hollywood's image of me was wrong and I knew it and I couldn't say anything about it, couldn't do anything about it. I was doing a lot of pictures close together and the pictures got very similar. If something was successful they'd try to recreate it the next time around. So I'd read the first four or five pages and I knew that it was just a different name with twelve new songs in it. The songs were mediocre in most cases. You couldn't get good songs. That's what might have made it seem like the indifference but I was never indifferent. I was so concerned. That's all I talked about. It worried me sick so I had to change it, which I did. I was obligated four years in advance. It's nobody fault maybe except my own. I didn't know what to do. I just felt I was obligated very heavy to do things I didn't fully believe in and it was very difficult. I mean, the contracts were signed four years in advance. So I had thought that they would try to get a new property for me or give me a chance to show some kind of acting ability or do a very interesting story but it did not change. It did not change and so I became very discouraged. They couldn't have paid me no amount of money in the world to make me feel any self satisfaction inside.
    —*Elvis on Tour,* interview

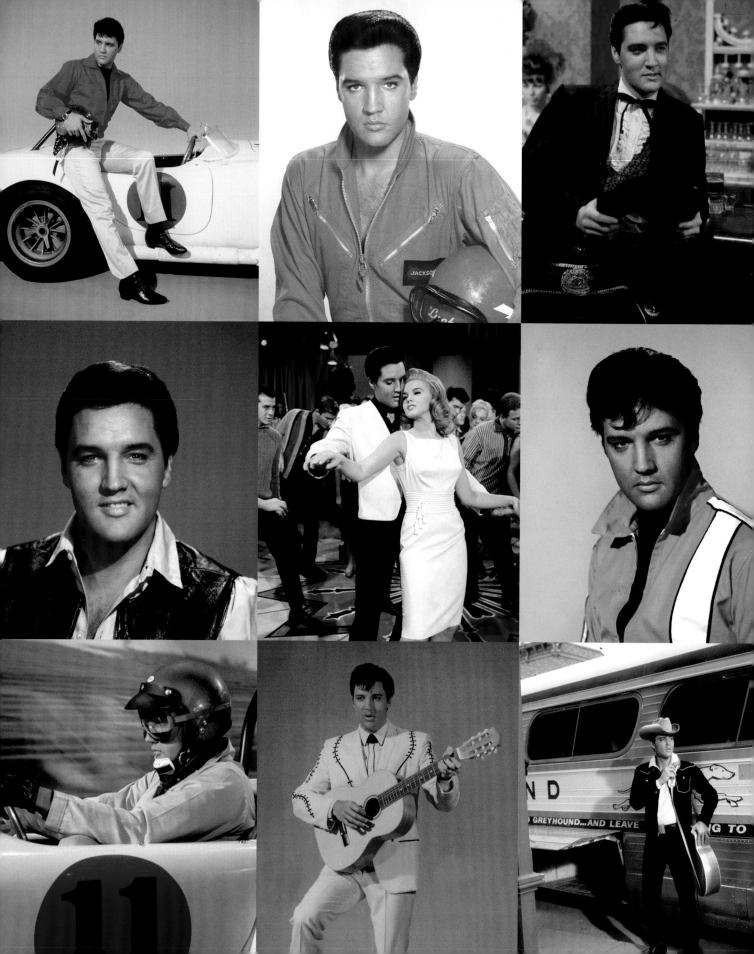

# RESURRECTION:
# THE '68 COMEBACK SPECIAL

With Elvis's movie career officially on the skids, coupled with a long cold streak without a big hit (1962's "Good Luck Charm" was his last number one single), it was clear that The King needed to find a vehicle which would reignite his stagnating career. Signed to star in his own television special, *Singer Presents Elvis* aired on NBC-TV on December 3, 1968 and garnered rapturous reviews from critics and fans alike. Now better known as the *'68 Comeback Special,* the show signaled a creative rebirth for Elvis and firmly planted the seeds for his triumphant return to the stage.

**STEVE binder** (director, *Singer Presents Elvis*): Colonel Parker was at a special party that Tom Sarnoff from NBC attended.

> **TOM SARNOff** (west coast vice-president of production and business affairs, NBC): The program department at NBC decided they wanted to do something with Elvis. I was introduced to the Colonel by John West, who was Vice President at NBC in charge of the West Coast and I reported to him.

**STEVE binder:** The two of them got into a conversation. The Colonel was interested in making a movie and the way they resolved it was Elvis would do a Christmas television special for NBC and then NBC would finance the movie, which became *Change of Habit*.

> **TOM SARNOff:** Any time the Colonel negotiated a deal he only knew one number and that was one million dollars. laughs But we ultimately signed Elvis to do the show for less than that. $250,000

**STEVE BINDER:** Everything was done without Elvis's knowledge. Bob Finkel, who was the executive producer on the special, said that even though there was a deal struck between the Colonel and Sarnoff, Elvis wasn't responding. He didn't want to do the television special. At the time I was doing a trilogy of specials. I did *Hallelujah, Leslie!*, a Leslie Uggams special for NBC and then I did *Petula*, the Petula Clark/Harry Belafonte special. That special was very controversial because in prime time television it broke the barrier between blacks and whites touching each other. There was a moment when Petula reached over and touched Harry's forearm while they were singing an anti-war duet called "Paths of Glory." This was during the time of the Vietnam War. That was the moment which broke the color line on prime-time variety television and it caused a lot of controversy. Our executive producer at NBC, Bob Finkel had this deal with Colonel Parker to do an Elvis special at NBC. Bob called me and said, "You know, every time I try to talk to Elvis Presley he always calls me Mr. Finkel and I realized even though we have a deal we're never gonna get this special made." He told me he read about my Petula/Belafonte incident and found out a little about my background "You're around the same age as Elvis.

I'm reading about you and you're sort of a rebel and it might be the perfect combination." He thought maybe here's a young guy that Elvis can relate to. I was 28 at the time.

I initially turned it down when Bob called me. At the time there was a very famous and legendary film producer named Walter Wanger. He had approached me about working on a movie with him. I had decided after the Petula Clark special that I was gonna move away from television and direct movies. My partner, Bones Howe, convinced me to do the Elvis special. Bones overheard the conversation and he said, "Steve, I engineered an album for Elvis and I think you guys would hit it off great. You're crazy if you turn this thing down." He said, "Why don't you meet with Bob Finkel and Elvis and see if you guys are compatible? I think you're making a big mistake if you don't do it."

So I called Bob Finkel and Bones and I went out to NBC to meet with him. This was without the Colonel or Elvis. Then Bones and I went out to MGM to meet the Colonel where he had his office and would hold court. While I was in his office, The Colonel gave me this tape called *Elvis's Special Christmas Program* that he circulated to all of the disc jockeys in America. It was a Christmas gift to the jocks featuring Elvis singing Christmas songs, both spiritual and traditional. Before I left he also gave me a "Snowman's League of America" club membership card and said, "You'll hear from us." The Colonel envisioned Elvis doing a Christmas special. In his mind, Elvis would come out and say, "Hello everybody" and at the end of the show he's say, "Goodnight everybody" and that would be the extent of his dialogue. He wanted Elvis to come out and sing 26 Christmas songs. I never had any intention of doing that kind of a show.

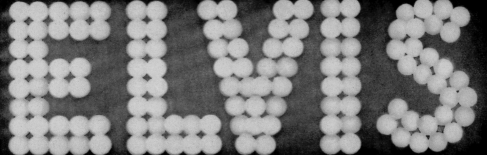

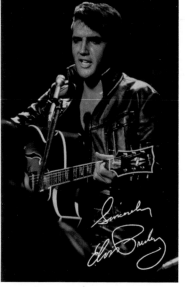

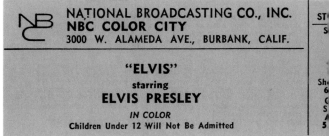

**bones howe** (music director, *Singer Presents Elvis*): Steve felt it was a terrible shame that Elvis had never been seen for the artist he really was. I told Steve, "Let's get in a room with Elvis and if he likes the idea he'll talk to the Colonel."

**steve binder:** Next thing I know Bob Finkel calls me and said, "The Colonel's approved you and you can meet with Elvis now." Bob asked, "How do you want to meet Elvis?" And I said, "I'd like him to meet us at our Binder/Howe offices on Sunset Boulevard". He arrived at around four in the afternoon in a Lincoln Continental with his entourage but he left them out in the lobby. When he walked in he said, "Hi Steve" and I said, "Hi Elvis". I never put Elvis on a pedestal. Fortunately I had a few credits behind me. I had worked with pretty major stars over the time frame to my Steve Allen experiences, *The T.A.M.I. Show* and *Hullabaloo*. The first question Elvis asked me when he walked into our offices on the Sunset Strip was, "Where do you think my career's at?" So I laughed at him and said, "I think it's in the toilet." He laughed out loud and said, "What do you mean?" And I said, "I haven't seen any hit records from you on the music charts." He laughed and said, "I agree with you." He appreciated my honesty. At that point the movie studios had burnt out on his movies and weren't paying him a million dollars to do these movies. So at the time Elvis's career was at a critical stage. And I think the Colonel recognized that. That's why he wanted to get another movie going and that's why he made the deal with NBC. Behind the scenes Elvis took on the Colonel. The Colonel could have fired me anytime he wanted to. He kept constantly screaming about doing a Christmas special. But Elvis kept saying, "Don't rock the boat, let these guys do what they want to do."

**priscilla presley:** Elvis was reluctant at first. Nothing had been done like this before. He knew he needed a change. He was so dissatisfied with his career. He really had no other choice. At the time, he didn't know if he had a career. His records weren't doing well. Musically he was a little in doubt. Then this wonderful concept came along and he went along for that ride. He would pace back and forth when he was nervous. "Is it the right thing to do?"
—PaleyFest08/Elvis '68 Comeback Special 40th Anniversary Celebration/March 14, 2008

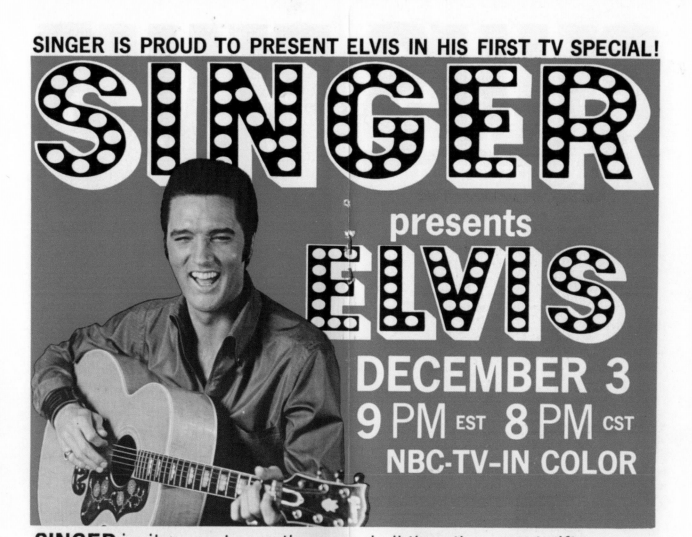

SINGER IS PROUD TO PRESENT ELVIS IN HIS FIRST TV SPECIAL!

# SINGER

## presents

# ELVIS

### DECEMBER 3
### 9 PM EST 8 PM CST
### NBC-TV-IN COLOR

**SINGER** invites you to see these—and all the other great gift ideas at your Singer Center

**TOUCH & SEW\*** sewing machines

Wide choice of cabinets too.

630/351

DON'T MISS OUR GREAT SELECTION OF HIT RECORDS BY TOP ARTISTS!

E-10

**SINGER ★ VACUUMS**

Choose from a wide variety of powerful upright vacuums and cannisters

U-44

*What's new for tomorrow is at* **SINGER** *today!*\*

\*A Trademark of THE SINGER COMPANY

**sandi miller** (fan): He was so worried that people wouldn't show up for the '68 Special that he was personally handing out tickets to the fans that waited outside his home.

**steve binder:** Elvis told me he was terrified of television because he hadn't performed in front of a live audience for almost ten years. He said, "My turf is a recording studio, not a television studio. I'm uncomfortable there." I said, "Then why don't you just make a record and I'll put pictures to it?" Weeks later he came to me and said, "It's those words that really made me trust you and be comfortable working with you because it made a lot of sense."

**tom sarnoff:** It was a coup to get Elvis to perform on television again. He did very little TV after he became a big star. He was a top star whose popularity was dimming. The Colonel thought, as we did, that the show would revitalize Elvis's career.

**priscilla presley:** Going through that time period with him and seeing how nervous he was and the process that he went through to get where he got was pretty amazing. He hadn't been in front of an audience for almost a decade. The process that he put himself through, does he take control? Does he trust this new director who was the hot director of the time? He was very trusting in that they came up with the decisions and he'd say, "Yes, I like it."

**chris hutchins** (European press representative for International Hotel/creative director, Tom Jones): The guys around him were his friends and they wanted to please him but they were frightened of Parker. They were frightened in encouraging Elvis to do anything, which Parker would have disapproved of so he was left in quite a quandary.

**steve binder:** We planned a big production show. The two guys who really brought the spine to the show, other than the improv, were the writers, Allan Blye and Chris Bearde. They locked themselves into a room in our offices and came out with a skeletal sketch of what turned out to be the special.

**chris bearde:** (co-writer, *Singer Presents Elvis*): The reality portion showed him performing onstage and the fictional part was the "Guitar Man" story, which sort of paralleled Elvis's life, telling the story of a guy who was a guitar man who grew up in a brothel and wound up being a superstar.

**steve binder:** There was a gospel section, which was a huge production segment with dancers and he worked with the Blossoms. And he planned on doing a medley of his hits with the full band.  That whole segment where he's in the boxing ring and wearing the black leather and singing the Billy Goldenberg medley of his hits was done live with the orchestra. That was the show we were doing.

**priscilla presley:** There's a moment where you see it in his eyes, he just came out. A lot of us thought he was just lost. He was not inspired, he had no motivation and things opened up for him and you could see it. That show saved his life. It saved his career. He got his confidence back. Music was what he lived for. Elvis was back to what he loved to do. And that was very pivotal for him in his career.

—PaleyFest08/Elvis '68 Comeback Special 40th Anniversary Celebration/March 14, 2008

**STEVE BINDER:** Priscilla Presley told me that Elvis would come home and say, "I'm not sure I know what's going on but I know something special's happening and I can't wait to get back to work again." When we actually went into physical production he lived in Dean Martin's old dressing room right next to Stage 4 at NBC where we shot the show. He made us clean out the dressing room and put a bed in. It was a lush dressing room with a living room but it was never meant to be a place you lived and slept in. There would have been no improv sections of the show without him living there because I would never have been able to be privy to seeing him after he finished work every day going into the dressing room spending hours unwinding by jamming, which was the great gift he gave all of us. I've always felt if you could record what goes on behind the door, and through the keyhole, it would be great. What he was doing in his dressing room was more exciting than what we were doing on the show and said, "We've got to get this on tape!" That was where he was sweating and his hair was messed up. He was just having a great time. This was something you'd never seen of Elvis, this raw power. I was bound and determined to capture that in the dressing room. I went to Colonel Parker and told him I wanted to bring a camera into the dressing room and he said, "Over my dead body." There was no way he was gonna allow that to happen. So I'd go in there and had a little Sony tape recorder and I just started recording it and listening to the guys jam for hours. It wasn't until I hounded the Colonel and got on his nerves every single day that finally out of frustration he said, "Okay, I'll tell you what to do. Recreate it out onstage if you want to but you're not getting into the dressing room with your cameras." So that's what I did.

When I told Elvis we were gonna recreate the improv on the stage he said, "If we're gonna do that I want you to bring in Scotty Moore and D.J. Fontana." They weren't involved in the show until we did the improv and we flew them in. They did it for Elvis. They didn't do it for the Colonel because the Colonel is what broke them up.

**D.J. FONTANA** (drums): We went out a few days earlier to see what was going on and watched Elvis rehearse the other parts of the show. It's a lot of work to do those shows. They had this stage set up; it was about the size of a boxing ring. They had all of us sitting up there. When we first went there they had a set of drums sitting there too. They said, "the drums are kind of taking up the whole stage and the lights are reflecting off the silver plated hardware they had." They spared them down and it didn't do any good. It was ruining the camera shot. And we said, "Well, just take 'em down." They said, "Well, what are you gonna do?" I said, "Well, I'll just play on the back of a guitar case. We've done this before."

**STEVE BINDER:** Right before we were gonna tape the sit down show my stage manager said, "You've got to talk to Elvis, he's in the makeup room." So I went out of the control booth and walked down to the makeup room. The minute I walked in Elvis asked the people in the room to leave. It was just the two of us in there. He said, "Steve, I've decided this is a stupid idea, I can't do it." And I said, "What do you mean you can't do it? There's an audience out there, we're ready to go." He said, "Well, to tell you the truth my mind's a blank. I don't now what I said and I don't remember any of the songs I sang. You have to go out there and tell the audience that I'm sick and I can't do it." And I said, "Elvis, I haven't asked you to so anything that you didn't want to do up to this point but now I'm not even asking you, you have to go out there. That audience is waiting for you. If you don't know what to sing or what to say, I'm gonna write down on a piece of white paper everything that I had remembered that you did in the dressing room." I wrote song titles down, and wrote stories that he told me like the Pan-Pacific story. During that show he said he could only move his little finger because the vice squad were there. I told him "Go out and say hello and if you can't remember anything say goodbye and come right back but you have to go out there." The minute he walked out there he was home. He forgot the cameras were following him and it was sensational. He went out there and he did basically two hours of improv and he could have done 200 hours probably.

**d.j. fontana:** The jam sessions were fun. There was no written dialogue that Elvis had to do or a list of tunes for him to do except for one, he had to do a Christmas song. He had a ball. We all had a good time, it was really fun. Everybody was cutting up and acting the fool like we always used to do, just sitting around the room talking.

**priscilla presley:** He didn't really come alive until he went on the stage in that little boxing ring. He was with people he felt comfortable, people he'd worked with in the past like D.J. Fontana and Scotty Moore. They were able to relate to each other and make jokes.

**marty lacker** (Memphis Mafia): Even though it was done in front of a controlled audience—the audience was filled with people he knew as well as fans off the street—that really got him excited about getting out on the road again.

**bones howe:** He came off the stage soaking wet from the black leather suit improv jam session and he was just bubbling over. He said, "Man, that was really fun!" I remember Elvis excitedly saying, "I want to talk to The Colonel. I want to go out and perform!"

**priscilla presley:** Then what started to unfold is he began to feel really comfortable and secure within himself. He began to feel confident again being in front of the fans. He decided then that he wanted to be back in front of a live audience. So you saw a whole era which took him into Vegas and then on tour in other cities.

**jerry schilling** (Memphis Mafia): The success of the '68 special gave him the confidence to perform live again. At this particular point in this career he wasn't at the top of his game. He hadn't had a big hit record for a long time and his movies weren't doing gangbuster business. Elvis was glad to get those long-term movie contracts over with. When you're not doing work that challenges you you're not at your best. He wasn't given the challenges worthy of his talent.

**tom jones:** Elvis always liked it if he had a challenge, if he had something new to do.

**steve binder:** After the show was finished, I showed him the master tape and we sat and watched it with his entourage. Then the second time he asked that just he and I sit in the room and watch it again. He was very proud of the '68 special. He looked at it as if he was watching someone else on the screen. I loved watching him because he was laughing in the right spots. He made me play it for him three times. Then he said, "I'm never gonna sing a song that I don't believe in again" and he also said "I'm never gonna do a movie I don't believe in." There was a lot of conversation between us. I said to him and it was just my gut reaction, "I hear you and I know you mean it Elvis but I'm not sure you're strong enough to do that." It turned out unfortunately to be very profound because Elvis never stood up to the Colonel for whatever reason.

**lisa marie presley:** That special happened the year that I was born. That was a very crucial moment for him. He was very afraid. He was just coming out of the movies and this was his first attempt to really take it all back on and I think he kicked its ass. When I finally saw the special I was incredibly proud and in awe. To this day I watch it and it's mind blowing. He literally showed everybody who was boss again.

**priscilla presley:** It was a history making special. At the time I remember watching him being nervous and then slowly regaining his confidence and starting to feel comfortable and then rediscovering himself and really wanting to go back on tour and being in front of the public again. It's a great journey to see him on that special and how much he enjoyed performing and how comfortable he felt. You see him emerge into this animal, this energetic, charismatic specimen. Seeing it today it's still as exciting and energetic. It's timeless.

**jerry schilling:** As important as Steve Binder was for the visual sense, Chips Moman was as important for the musical side. That was the beauty of the sessions with Chips. Chips said, "I've got a stack of records that your publishers brought in and that you own the publishing and I've got another stack over here of hit records and you don't own anything. Which one do you want to record?" Elvis said, "Look, I wanna go out on the road, I want hit records." So it was a combination of the success of the '68 special and the American Sound sessions, which generated hits like "Suspicious Minds' and "In the Ghetto," that really set the stage for Elvis to return to live performance

**steve binder:** The '68 special proved to Elvis that he wasn't a has-been. After the special, I think Elvis really wanted to go out there and take advantage of the comeback and test some new waters.

# RETURN TO THE STAGE

A day after the TV special aired, Mike Jahn, a writer with the *New York Times*, broke a national story that Elvis was planning a return to the concert stage.

Mike Jahn
New York Times
December 4, 1968

Elvis Presley, with one eye to the increasing interest in old-style rock and the other to his decreasing income from movie roles, is making plans for personal nationwide appearances. Mr. Presley has not appeared before a live audience since 1961. According to business associates of the singer, his income from the moves has been decreasing. Tom Diskin, a spokesman for Col. Tom Parker, Mr. Presley's manager, declined to give an exact figure but said that the decrease was significant to cause Mr. Presley and his manager to consider personal appearances. "For the time that goes into it," Mr. Diskin said," it's more profitable for him to appear in public. It takes Elvis 15 weeks time to make a movie on the average. If he appears for 10 weeks, one concert a week, at $100,000 each he can do much better. In personal appearances these days $100,000 a concert is not an unrealistic figure."

## JOHN L. SCOTT

## Elvis Billed for Rare Stage Stint

Elvis Presley, who has made only three major stage appearances in 13 years, begins a four-week engagement next Thursday night in Kirk Kerkorian's International Hotel in Las Vegas.

The man whose phenomenal recording career has earned about 50 gold records (each representing a million discs sold) and who is now referred to respectfully by young pop singers as "the old man," fulfilled a commitment in another Vegas hotel in 1956, rocked the staid Pan Pacific in Los Angeles to its foundations in 1957, and appeared at the Battleship Arizona Memorial in Pearl Harbor in 1961.

Presley's activities in recording and motion picture mediums, however, have brought him fame and fortune. It was actually his third film, "Jailhouse Rock," that nailed down his claim to screen stardom. Now he has about 30 major movies to his credit, including his most recent release, "Change of Habit."

Presley's current "In the Ghetto" recording is one of 1969's four top sellers. It recently hit the 1.5 million mark.

The star will appear in the International's massive 2,000-seat main showroom. On the same bill will be comedian Sammy Shore and a group called the Sweet Inspirations.

Barbra Streisand completes her engagement there Wednesday evening.

*Elvis Presley*

## Elvis Signs Pact for Date in Las Vegas

Elvis Presley signed a contract Wednesday to make his first major stage appearance in 13 years. He'll star at the Las Vegas International Hotel next summer, following Barbra Streisand, whose pact was revealed 10 days ago.

With the exception of an appearance at the Battleship Arizona Memorial at Pearl Harbor in 1961, Presley's stage work has been limited to one engagement in 1956 when he played another Las Vegas supper club.

The singer-actor has been busy doing films and recording. His next picture will be "Change of Habit," for Universal release.

Presley flew to Las Vegas for the signing after several months of negotiation between entertainment director Bill Miller and Presley's manager, Colonel Parker.

—JOHN SCOTT

Buoyed by the rave reviews that greeted the *Singer Presents Elvis* TV special, Elvis was ready to return to the concert stage.

**elvis presley:** I missed the closeness of a live audience. So just as soon as I got out of the movie contracts I started to do live performances again. (New York City press conference, June 9, 1972)

**chris hutchins:** I met Elvis in '65 with the Beatles. At that meeting the Beatles said to Elvis, "Why don't you get back on the road and stop making those crappy films?" And he was offended by it. I knew how pent up he was about the fact that they'd taken his crown and he wanted to get it back. He felt powerless to do anything about it because Parker just wanted him to make movies, that's where the money was. That frustration came through every single time I saw him. He just really wanted to get back to performing. Colonel Parker told me that Elvis kept bugging him to go back on the road and Colonel kept talking about the films. It was a battle between the two.

In '68, I arranged for Elvis to see Tom Jones in Vegas. I called Joe Esposito and said, "Bring Elvis up" because I knew Elvis had all of Tom's records. Joe called me back and said "Okay, get us a table for ten". He was the moody Elvis then, the dark glasses and little cigar.

**tom jones:** Elvis came to see me perform in 1968 at the Flamingo Hotel, which I was thrilled about. When we were talking afterwards he said, "The reason I've come to see you is because I'm thinking of performing live again." He tried to crack Vegas in the '50s and they weren't ready for rock and roll then. So he always wanted to go back to Vegas and become a success there. He felt I was the closest thing to him and had a similar stage presence. If I could make it there he felt that he could too. So he wanted to see me work and saw what I did onstage.

**nicholas naff** (director of advertising and publicity, International Hotel): Elvis watched the way Tom Jones moved very carefully. He wasn't interested in singing like Tom but more about studying how he moved. He also was interested in Tom's connection with a female audience. Tom Jones was selling sex appeal and Elvis was selling purity and innocence. Of course, he had a sex appeal too but it wasn't as blatant as Tom Jones. It was more a byproduct of his personality.

**nicholas naff:** What Elvis got from Tom was the trick of working the Vegas stage. Tom showed him you have to be sensual in a way that gets through to the over-30s. Tom gave Elvis the freeze poses at the end of the songs, the trick of wiping the sweat with a cloth and then throwing it out to the house. (*Las Vegas Life*, January 2000/Neal Karlen)

**chris hutchins:** He had a great rapport with Tom. Tom said to him, "Why don't you get back to playing live? That's what you do best" And because he really liked Tom and respected him he listened and agreed.

**tom jones:** He told me, "You've given me the confidence to make a comeback in Vegas," which he did in '69.

**emilio muscelli** (head showroom maître d', International Hotel, 1969-1977): I first met Elvis at the Flamingo Hotel in 1968 when he came to see a show by Tom Jones. He didn't know but I knew they were contracting with Tom Parker for Elvis to play Las Vegas. I told him, "One year from now I'm gonna be your maître d' and he said, "Aw c'mon, get out of here, that's not true." But it was true. A year later he came in to play the International Hotel and I told him, "See, I'm your maître d'." (laughs)

# international hotel: the back story

The newly constructed International Hotel was the largest hotel in Las Vegas at the time and would be the site of Elvis's "Sin City" comeback shows.

**bruce banke:** The International was slated to be the largest convention-oriented hotel in the world. In early 1967, Kerkorian purchased the Las Vegas Downs horse race track located on 80 acres of prime real estate directly adjacent to the mammoth, county-owned Las Vegas Convention Center.

**nicholas naff:** Kirk Kerkorian bought the Flamingo Hotel to staff up for the International. He was a man who had sufficient capital to build a hotel that was larger than anything on the Strip before. It was going to be the largest hotel constructed up until that time.

**bruce banke** (assistant director of publicity and advertising, International Hotel): The International Hotel was built by the millionaire airline tycoon Kirk Kerkorian and it was situated just two blocks off the famed Las Vegas Strip on Paradise Road.

**bobby morris** (orchestra leader, Bobby Morris Orchestra): It was the first hotel that wasn't on the main thoroughfare of the Las Vegas strip.

**bruce banke:** Critics thought he was crazy to build a major gaming property two blocks off the Strip.

**kirk kerkorian** (owner, International Hotel): Being off the Strip wasn't a problem. In fact, it made the International that much more special. It was the only hotel like it in the world.

**lou toomin** (personal friend of Alex Shoofey): The original concept was two separate 1500 room towers but that never materialized. They built the 1500 room tower and expanded it through the years and where the other tower was supposed to be they built a convention center.

**bruce banke:** Las Vegas had been built on high rollers, nickel slot players, top name entertainment and $1.95 dinner buffets. The days of the huge 50,000-75,000-person conventions were far in the future, but Kerkorian saw them coming. He started putting together an expert staff to operate his $60 million, 30-story hotel which would open in less than two years. By contrast, Kerkorian's 5,000 room MGM Grand Hotel in Las Vegas that opened in the early '90s, cost $1.85 billion! His first step was to hire Alex Shoofey, the very successful executive vice president of Del Webb's Sahara Hotel, to run the hotel side of the 1,519-room project. Jimmy Newman who was a highly respected gaming executive was named vice president of casino operations.

International Hotel owner Kirk Kerkorian

Shoofey raided his own staff and hired 73 Sahara executives and key employees to form the nucleus of the International's staff. Kerkorian's next move was a masterpiece in pre-planning. He bought Bugsy Siegel's pride and joy, the run down, 777-room Flamingo Hotel, located in the middle of the Strip, directly across from glitzy Caesar's Palace, to use as a training site for his entire International staff. The plan was to sell the Flamingo in 1969, and move all of its employees into the International just prior to opening. Shoofey and Newman spent about $2 million in remodeling, and turned the 20-year old property around, making it into a big money maker. Kerkorian decided to keep the Flamingo, causing considerable problems for the staff. Instead of picking up and moving into the International a month before opening, the entire executive staff had to find replacements for themselves and their employees to continue running the Flamingo. Recruiting offices were opened from Miami to San Francisco. The Las Vegas market was not large enough at that time to handle so many new jobs.

**loanne miller parker** (secretary for Alex Shoofey, president of the International Hotel, and Colonel Parker's widow): Alex Shoofey was a detail man. He was a perfectionist. He wanted everything to be the best. He wanted the best soaps, he wanted the best towels. He wanted the guests to feel pampered as though they'd come to a place that was really first class.

**kirk kerkorian:** Before it opened I brought in a lot of important people to look at it like (Aristotle) Onassis.

# 2 New Hotels Open in Vegas in July

**INTERNATIONAL CUISINE... IN A CORPS OF FASCINATING RESTAURANTS!** All the splendid flavors of far-away world—cuisine and service equally sup[...] right here in International Territory, in our com[...] five International restaurants. ✤ Our **Japanese Re[...]** for example, offers you the delicate flavors of Far [...] cooking. Amidst sliding doors and exquisite wate[...] Japanese cooks prepare an unusual menu of aut[...] Japanese dishes, and waitresses in picturesque ki[...] serve you with Oriental grace. ✤ But if you're in [...] mood for a really hearty meal, you'll try our **Ba[...] Restaurant.** Here, too, the motif is carried out in [...] furnishings and embellishments. A *gemuetlich* m[...] seats you. And a waiter in full Bavarian costume ta[...] order. The food is expertly prepared by continent[...] masters of the culinary art. ✤ The same goes for [...] **Italian Restaurant** and our **Mexican Restaurant.** Th[...] are Neopolitan and early Californian, but the coo[...] out of this world. Not quite the same as you'd fin[...] own home town. For at the International, the ac[...] on the rare, the unusual. These restaurants were [...] to give you a different experience in savory dini[...] ✤ Finally, the International's **Gourmet Restauran[...]** ultimate in epicurean eating from all earth's corners. Defiantly we say, in fineness of food or service, the country has none to offer that is better. ✤ **A Marvelous Coffee Shop, Too!** Of course, when it comes to a snack or a full course meal in the more regular sense, the International has a beautifully designed coffee shop, open 24 hours a day. It seats 500, but you'd never believe it from the plush booths and intimacy of seating arrangement. It's a joy to be in it!

**THE INTERNATIONAL HOTEL IS HERE... AND LAS VEGAS WILL NEVER BE THE SAME!** As soon as you drive up to the new International Hotel, you know you're on International Territory. It's different. It's visibly exciting. All the flags of the free world are blowing in the breeze. ✤ The doorman who opens your car isn't a doorman. He's a French gendarme. And the International's lobby isn't a lobby. It's more like the Palace Versailles. With a desk that's 100 feet long. Where they hand you an International Passport as you register. ✤ When they take you up to your floor, you blink in astonishment. It's as if you're on the Continent. Or in the Orient. For each floor is done in international decor. Spanish. French provincial. Oriental. And your room carries out the motif. ✤ Go to dine, and you find 5 great International restaurants to choose from. Including Italian. Japanese. Bavarian. Western American. Each with its own staff, chef, bill of fare and national cuisine. ✤ Then drop into one of the 3 fabulous International theatres, and there's another outstanding International Star to entertain you. Like Barbra Streisand. Or Elvis Presley. Or see a lavishly magnificent musical. ✤ There's even an International Youth Hotel for your children. And the world's largest swimming pool. A casino that's as glittering and romantic as Monte Carlo's. And the championship 18-hole International Golf Course nearby. ✤ Is it any wonder Las Vegas has been declared International Territory? Or any wonder Las Vegas will never be the same?

**MYRAM BORDERS** (writer, *Nevada State Journal*): There was a war going on between Kirk Kerkorian who was opening the International Hotel and Howard Hughes' people who were opening the Landmark Hotel across the street. Both the International and Landmark were multi-story buildings and were the tallest hotels in the city. We didn't have a lot of those kinds of buildings back then. So the International was vying with the Landmark to open first. Ultimately, I think the International opened a day earlier.

**EMILIO MUSCELLI:** The International Hotel opened on July 2, 1969. The hotel had 1500 rooms when it first opened. Then a few years later it expanded to 3,173 rooms.

**KIRK KERKORIAN:** At the time, it was the largest hotel in the world and was first class all the way. It had beautiful luxurious suites and the largest showroom in Vegas. I named it the International Hotel because it felt international to me. It worked too because it attracted foreign visitors from around the world.

**LOANNE MILLER PARKER:** It was an amalgam of all the countries. There was a Parisian bar. The steakhouse was representative of the West. There was a gourmet room that had an Egyptian theme, an Italian restaurant and the Bavarian room.

**JOE ESPOSITO** (Memphis Mafia): A lot of people didn't know if the hotel would make it because it was so big and such an expensive project for its time but it did extremely well.

L -R, International hotel President Alex Shoofey, Elvis, talent booker Bill Miller

# "a fortune won and lost on every deal"...

Elvis would sign a lucrative deal with the International Hotel, which would pay him a then unprecedented fee of $125,000 per week. On July 31, 1969, Elvis would perform his first live show in eight years since taking part in two 1961 charity performances in Memphis and Honolulu.

**bruce banke:** Kerkorian told Shoofey, "I want to headline only the biggest names in the showroom and and I mean NEW faces in Las Vegas!" Shoofey knew there was only one person in the world capable of handling that type of assignment and that was the legendary Bill Miller. He was the former owner of the famed Bill Miller's Riviera nightclub located just over the George Washington Bridge in Fort Lee, New Jersey. He was sixty-five year's old at the time, gray haired and perpetually sun tanned and enjoying semi-retirement in the Caribbean. He was immediately hired and took over the entertainment duties at the Flamingo while looking ahead at the monumental job of finding fresh new faces to open the International. Kerkorian was adamant when he said, "Sinatra, Sammy (Davis Jr.) and Dean Martin are great, established Las Vegas entertainers— but I want exciting new faces at the International!" Bill Miller told Alex Shoofey, "There are only two names out there big enough to open this hotel. Presley and Streisand." Barbra Streisand was a proven commodity, having just won an Academy Award for *Funny Girl*. Elvis was still soaring after his '68 Singer Show, but

had not done another major concert in many years. Ironically, both had played Las Vegas earlier; Barbra, in 1963 as an opening act for Liberace at the Riviera, and Elvis, for Shecky Greene at the New Frontier in 1956.

**nicholas naff:** In the case of a new hotel, because entertainment is so significant in Las Vegas, naturally they wanted to open with the biggest star and offer a show that would draw the most people and generate the most publicity. As the hotel developed and it came down to the point of selecting entertainers for the hotel, we had a major meeting where we were going to decide who'd be the opening star entertainment. Bill Miller, Alex Shoofey and I were among the people at that meeting. They put five major entertainers before us and asked us to select the one that would be the opening act for the new hotel. Barbra Streisand, Elvis Presley and Nancy Sinatra were among the names mentioned.

**bruce banke:** Miller was leaning toward Elvis to open the property. He put in a call to his old friend, Colonel Tom Parker and flew in to meet him in Los Angeles.

**alex shoofey** (president, International Hotel): We knew Colonel Parker from way back. The Colonel was around during the Sahara days. He was a very good friend of Milton Prell. As a matter of a fact, Elvis got married at the Aladdin when Milton Prell was running it. I got to know him through Milton Prell. It was the entertainment director (Bill Miller) who contacted him the first time. Everybody was competing for the top dog. I don't know if everybody was capable of paying because we had a room that seated more than 1,000 people. (UNLV Oral History Research Center, March 2003)

**bill miller** (talent booker, International Hotel): We finally got (Elvis) on one condition. (Colonel Tom) Parker didn't want him to open in that big 2,000-seat theater. (*Las Vegas Review Journal*)

**alex shoofey:** The Colonel said, "Listen Alex, get somebody else to do the opening, I don't want Elvis to do it. This is the first time he's coming in." (UNLV Oral History Research Center, March 2003)

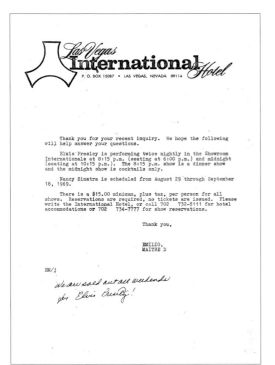

Thank you for your recent inquiry. We hope the following will help answer your questions.

Elvis Presley is performing twice nightly in the Showroom Internationale at 8:15 p.m. (seating at 6:00 p.m.) and midnight (seating at 10:15 p.m.). The 8:15 p.m. show is a dinner show and the midnight show is cocktails only.

Nancy Sinatra is scheduled from August 29 through September 18, 1969.

There is a $15.00 minimum, plus tax, per person for all shows. Reservations are required, no tickets are issued. Please write the International Hotel, or call 702 732-5111 for hotel accommodations or 702 734-7777 for show reservations.

Thank you,

EMILIO,
MAITRE D

EM/j

*We are sold out all weekends for Elvis Presley!*

**bruce banke:** He told Bill Miller, "You let Miss Streisand do that. We'll come in a month later after you get all the kinks worked out."

**bill miller:** So I went to work on Barbra Streisand. She was on her way to Europe when I got her to sign the contract. (*Las Vegas Review Journal*)

**nicholas naff:** Barbra Streisand was ultimately selected to be the first act to open the hotel. One of the reasons we picked her was just recently she had won an Academy Award for *Funny Girl*. So we knew we wouldn't have to work really hard to publicize her. She already was a star and it was also timely. That influenced going with her rather than Elvis or Nancy Sinatra.

**alex shoofey:** Reservations were coming in from all over the world for Elvis Presley's coming engagement. They were pouring in. It assisted the opening because of that. Those phones were ringing off the hook for reservations for Elvis Presley. Barbra (Streisand) was offered an interest in the hotel. Five bucks for a piece, that was stock. She would get 20,000 shares of stocks for zero. Needless to say that went up to $100 in a very short period of time. Barbara was sharp. When she was offered the stock, she took it, no questions asked. That stock went sky-high after that. She made a ton of money. That was the reason she agreed (to do the opening), because of the stock. I even tried to get the Colonel to buy some for Elvis and he said, "No, I don't believe in that shit, Alex." (UNLV Oral History Research Center, March 2003)

**joe esposito:** Colonel Parker told Elvis it was a great deal. Elvis was a little nervous because the first time he played Vegas back in '56 he wasn't very successful. But Colonel talked him into it and he said, "Okay, let's do it."

**bruce banke:** Shortly after the agreement was OK'd, the Colonel arranged for Elvis to fly into Las Vegas on February 26, 1969, for a "contract signing" media event. Miller and Shoofey decided to hold it on the showroom stage at the unfinished International. The event was held on stage in the unfinished showroom which was still showing bare steel beams. It was a "hard hat" construction area but no one was about to tell Elvis to put on a heavy metal construction hat.

**loanne miller parker:** Colonel and Alex Shoofey were in the hotel coffee shop and they worked out figures for the deal on a table cloth.

**alex shoofey:** He (the Colonel) says, "Now tell me again. You'll give me the same money for the five years?" And I said, "Absolutely." I mean, this was unheard of that anybody would sign for five years for the same amount of money, no increase. So he took the tablecloth, and he signed it. (Mr. Rock & Roll documentary, 1999)

**loanne miller parker:** That tablecloth is now housed in the archives at Graceland.

**bruce banke:** In mid April of '69 a formal contract was signed calling for Elvis to perform two shows a night for four weeks in 1969 and then do two four-week engagements a year starting in 1970.

**colonel tom parker:** Elvis got more money during the period we played here (Las Vegas) than any artist in town, Liberace was getting $50,000; he was getting $125,000. (ABC-TV, "Nightline", January 8, 1993)

**bruce banke:** He would receive a half a million dollars per engagement. Colonel negotiated a revised contract in 1972, in 1973, and again in December 1976 for Elvis to receive $375,000 for his 15 concerts.

**lou toomin:** Alex Shoofey changed the face of show business when he signed Elvis and Barbra Streisand because those were big figure contracts. They were making barrels full of money, much more than any other entertainer was receiving. He was willing to take a risk.

**nicholas naff:** Colonel Parker moved into Las Vegas months before the International Hotel opened. Colonel Parker would come to the hotel quite frequently and he'd mostly stop by my office, which was next to Alex Shoofey's, because I was handling advertising and publicity. I saw a lot of him. After I'd finished my term at the hotel and left, he married my secretary (Loanne Miller). I say that only to indicate how frequently he was in my office so that's how he got to know her.

**bruce banke:** The unfinished International Hotel officially opened at 10 AM. on an extremely hot July 2, 1969. The interiors of the rooms on the upper 15 floors weren't even completed by opening day, compounding the problems faced by the brand new property.

**kirk kerkorian:** We opened that hotel with Barbra Streisand in the main showroom.

**bruce banke:** Barbra's opening performance was well received with actor Cary Grant, who was a close friend of Kerkorian's, serving as master of ceremonies before an invitation-only audience. Of course, as with any project that large, there were minor problems with the stage equipment and the sound system, but they were quickly corrected. On opening night a heavy sand bag fell from the ceiling loft, hitting the stage a few feet from Barbra. She never missed a beat. "See what happens when you build places this big with a GI loan?" she told the audience. Peggy Lee was also very successful as the opening headliner in the hotel's showroom-sized, 500-seat lounge. But the hotel's opening with Barbra was nothing compared to what took place 29 days later.

**myram borders:** Streisand bombed in Vegas. A week after she opened her handlers called in a lot of national media hoping to increase her exposure. The reason that she bombed certainly wasn't because of her talent. It was because the hotel wasn't quite finished. I don't think it met her standard of perfection and she talked more than she sang and that was not acceptable.

**kirk kerkorian:** Elvis followed Barbra in the main showroom. I don't know of any hotel that went that big on entertainment. The rock musical "Hair" was in the other showroom and the opening lounge act was Ike and Tina Turner. (*Las Vegas Review Journal*)

**joe esposito:** We all went and saw Barbra's closing show. Elvis went backstage and they had a nice conversation. The next day she came to Elvis's opening show.

# CONTACTING THE BAND MEMBERS

For his first live shows in almost ten years, Elvis reached out to long-time band mates, guitarist Scotty Moore and drummer D.J. Fontana, who turned down the offer. Intent on putting together the hottest band to play the Strip, Elvis contacted guitar legend James Burton and plans were put in motion to assemble a batch of seasoned pros. Better known as the TCB band, this tight and exciting ensemble would include guitarist John Wilkinson, bassist Jerry Scheff, drummer Ronnie Tutt, and pianist Larry Muhoberac, who would be replaced after the first engagement by Glen D. Hardin. Also on hand were two backing vocal groups, the gospel quartet, the Imperials and an R&B female act, the Sweet Inspirations.

**JERRY SCHILLING:** When he was planning to go back out on the road in Vegas he was looking to put together musicians and singers that reflected his entire body of work and influences. The rhythm section harkened back to his early days and the Imperials showed off his love for gospel music. The Sweet Inspirations' style was the R&B and soul music that we got turned on to through Dewey Phillips radio show, *Red, Hot & Blue*. That music was exciting, it was colorful, and it was different. Elvis had so many influences but I think as far as a performer it was totally R&B.

**SCOTTY MOORE:** D.J. (Fontana), the Jordanaires and I were all contacted about the 1969 Las Vegas shows. We were called by Tom Diskin, who was the Colonel's assistant. We were offered five weeks in Las Vegas that included rehearsal and shows at $500 per man a week. At that time, I owned a studio, Music City Recorders, in Nashville. D.J. was playing two to three sessions per day in Nashville and the Jordanaires had 40 sessions on the books in those five weeks. Economically, we simply could not afford to go to Las Vegas for $500 a week. In addition to that, we knew the offer was low because management wanted new personnel.

**MARTY LACKER** (Memphis Mafia): In early '69, Elvis went into American Sound studios in Memphis with Chips Moman and he was really into those sessions. Out of those sessions came such hits as "Suspicious Minds," "In The Ghetto" and "Don't Cry Daddy". One day we were in the control room and Elvis shocked me when he said to Chips, "Listen, I'm gonna be opening in Vegas in August and I'd like for these guys (American Studio band) to be my backup group." He also wanted Chips out there to handle the sound. I didn't think there was any way it was gonna happen because they couldn't pay Chips and the band more money than what they'd make in the studio. Remember, these guys were turning out hit after hit. In six years they had 150 hit records. But Chips said, "Yeah, I think we'll do that." Unfortunately, Colonel Parker was so upset about losing control of that session that he would never let that happen.

**elvis presley:** I wanted musicians who could play any kind of music. All of the musicians are all handpicked. I auditioned musicians for days and days, drummers and guitar players. I said, "Who's the best guitar player around?" And they said, "Glen Campbell and James Burton." I said, "Well, Campbell's out, he's on his own so James Burton." There's a lot of good men around me, it was just a matter of finding them. They all just fit in and fortunately they knew most of my songs. I wanted voices behind me to help add to the fullness of the sound and dynamics of the show. (*Elvis on Tour*, interview)

**johnny rivers:** Way before Elvis ever hired James Burton, we'd get together and listen to records and jam on stuff like "Travelin' Man." We loved all the old Ricky Nelson records because we loved the band that was on those records. And we loved the lead guitar lines and riffs that James Burton played. When Elvis got his band together for his comeback in Vegas James must have been in the back of his mind.

**jerry schilling:** Elvis had a lot of respect for James Burton. He knew his history and had watched him on *The Ozzie and Harriet Show*.

**james burton** (lead guitar, TCB Band): Elvis called me in '68 to do that Comeback Special but I wasn't available. Elvis had an offer to play Vegas and he called me and asked if I'd consider working with him and put the band together. We talked for about three and a half hours on the phone. In our conversation he said, "Man, I watched the *Ozzie and Harriett* TV show just to see you play guitar and Ricky sing." He loved guitar playing. Out roots were very similar. He's a southern boy from Mississippi and I'm from Shreveport, Louisiana and we liked the same type of music. At the time, I was very busy doing four or five sessions a day, seven days a week. But I ultimately made the decision to do it and it worked out great. When he called me, Elvis wanted me to find players that could play different styles and could improvise. He asked me to handpick the band and said, "Go and get who you want and I'll fly out in few weeks and we'll have auditions." He believed in me and respected my opinion and I wasn't gonna let him down. I wanted musicians that could play with the same energy, feeling and soul that Elvis had. I had all the freedom in the world 'cause our styles were very similar. He just gave me all the leverage I needed. Elvis knew what he wanted. Everything we played, everything he sang, it all came together. It was like a marriage and it was like that onstage too. We were out in Vegas twice a year, playing for a whole month, two shows a night, seven nights a week. Not many singers can do that but Elvis rose to the occasion and pulled it off.

**glen d. hardin** (piano, TCB band): I was entirely too busy at the time to be a part of Elvis's band for his '69 shows; I joined the band in 1970. I was arranging music for everyone from Dean Martin to the First Edition, Kenny Rogers's band.

**larry muhoberac** (piano, TCB band): I first worked with Elvis in the early '60s. I was musical director for two benefit shows he did in Memphis (the Ellis Auditorium). That was the first time I saw Elvis play live. I also worked on a few of his soundtrack albums (*Paradise, Hawaiian Style, Frankie and Johnny, Speedway* and *Viva Las Vegas*).

**james burton:** In '69, I was doing a jazz album with Shorty Rogers, who was a great producer and musician and Larry Muhoberac was playing piano.

**larry muhoberac:** Tom Diskin called me and said that Elvis was gonna do some live shows in Vegas and asked if I wanted to be a part of the group. Of course, I said yes immediately. I didn't have to go through an audition, they already knew what I could do and the same goes for James Burton.

**jerry schilling:** I spent a lot of time at those rehearsals. Elvis was enjoying just being with musicians again. He was enjoying the freedom of it.

**john wilkinson** (rhythm guitar, TCB band): He was so excited about starting up again.

**jerry schilling:** All the big session players and live players were put on notice that Elvis was putting together a band and they were all coming to the auditions. He wasn't just sitting there watching people play. He was out there singing songs with energy and fun.

**james burton:** We'd audition with songs like "Mystery Train," "That's All Right, Mama" and "Love Me Tender." Elvis trusted me and had confidence in my judgment. We were definitely thinking on the same page. In the rehearsals he'd do a song maybe three or four times and if it didn't sound right we'd move on to another song. After the auditions Elvis would ask me what I thought and I gave him my opinion. I brought in Richie Frost, who was my drummer who played with Ricky Nelson. He was a studio guy who worked with a lot of great entertainers. He played so great at the rehearsal. He played it perfect. Afterwards Richie came to me and said, "I really appreciate this but I'm fixin' to retire and I don't want to work this hard (laughs)." He could see the energy that Elvis expected.

**larry muhoberac:** We went through many auditions for bass players and drummers. James and I were there and Elvis, of course. I knew every good drummer in Hollywood, but Tom Diskin got them in there. We got to number seventy, all really good drummers, but none of them were exactly right. We were getting toward the end of the line and they were gonna make a decision on a drummer. I called Ron Tutt, who I'd worked with in Dallas and said, "I know you want to leave Dallas and do something else. Get on out here if you want the job with Elvis."

**ronnie tutt** (drummer, TCB band): The same night (I auditioned) there was a guy named Gene Pello who was the drummer for all the Motown sessions. He was well known in town and I was totally unknown. I just flew in the day before, because of Larry Muhoberac's recommendation. They'd been auditioning drummers for weeks and they still weren't happy. It was the last night and I came in there and brought my drums, I hauled them in on the airline. (The Elvis Touch/July 2002)

**ronnie tutt:** I set them up, this drummer walks in (Gene Pello), goes to my drums and starts playing around, thinking they are a rental. He starts playing and somebody says, "Hey, that's that guy's set." So he says, "Hey man, is it okay if I play your drums?" And I said, "Well, I guess so." As the evening started, they'd play a song, and I could see everybody going, "Yeah, we found the guy!" (Elvis Australia/www.elvis.com/au/Arjan Deelen)

**ronnie tutt:** They obviously were very tired of auditioning drummers and they'd found somebody who played well. So all this transpired before my eyes and I'm sinking slowly, going lower and lower into my seat. I'd brought my drums all the way from Texas and I'm not even going to get the chance to play. (The Elvis Touch/July 2002)

**RONNIE TUTT:** Larry (Muhoberac) goes over to Colonel Parker and says, "You know, this guy that you just bought a ticket for, he's right over there." And that got his attention because it cost some money! (laughs) The Colonel went over to Elvis, and I could tell they were all reluctant to play more. But they did. (Elvis Australia/www.elvis.com/au/Arjan Deelen)

**RONNIE TUTT:** So I get up and play, and instantly Elvis and I had this rapport, this eye contact. (The Elvis Touch/July 2002)

**JERRY SCHILLING:** He played at the audition and then they tried a couple of the other drummers. Elvis came over to me, Joe (Esposito) and Charlie (Hodge) and said, "I wanna see that big guy on the drums again." So he went back out there with Ronnie. I don't remember what song they were doing but Elvis said, "Accentuate what I'm doing, Ronnie." It's what D.J. (Fontana) used to do because D.J. had the background from playing burlesque shows and he knew how to accentuate a move.

**RONNIE TUTT:** I emulated and accented everything he did instinctively. Every move, almost like a glorified stripper! (Elvis Australia/www.elvis.com/au/Arjan Deelen)

**JAMES BURTON:** Ronnie got on the drums and he played so good, smoke was flyin' off the bass drum and hi-hat. (laughs)

**JERRY SCHILLING:** Elvis came back and said, "I need one guy onstage who has my temperament and this guy has it."

**RONNIE TUTT:** He said "You know Ronnie, those other drummers were good, but he was doing his own thing and you were watching me all the time. I knew that I could look around at anytime and I could see you, and you could see me. That's what I wanted." Like I told him one time, I needed to have that rapport as well. (The Elvis Touch/July 2002)

**SONNY WEST** (Memphis Mafia): Elvis made Ronnie a much better drummer because of all the different types of music he did, from the ballads to the up tempo songs. Elvis ignited something in him as a player. Elvis loved the way that Ronnie was tuned into him.

People asked Elvis, "Why don't you get a great session drummer like Hal Blaine?" And he said, "He's fantastic but I need a banger, not a seasoned session player." He wanted someone who could bring some rawness to the table and that was Ronnie.

**JERRY SCHEFF** (bass, TCB band): Up to that time I basically thought that jazz and classical was what was happening. Even though I was playing pop and rock before that, I wasn't playing rock Elvis's way, and playing with guys like James (Burton) and Ronnie (Tutt) really opened my mind. It was an education. I went down the first night (to the audition), but I wasn't going to take the job. I said to my wife: "I'm just gonna check this guy out." She didn't like him either. I went in, and it was just the band and him. I had always loved the blues, and he sang some blues songs. There was just something about the way he sang, and also the way he'd interact, that was really good. It was the musical communication and personal communication. He was just really nice to us. It was fun to play, you know. "Let's do this," clowning around, "Let's play that." I don't remember him every saying to any of us: "I don't like that, don't play that. Play it this way." (Elvis Australia/www.elvis.com/au/Arjan Deelen)

**larry muhoberac:** Jerry was the perfect bass player for Elvis. He had the right feel and style that Elvis liked.

**james burton:** He had a lot of strong energy in his playing, just a fluid player who really played great. He always voiced the right notes and played with the right feel whether it was rock and roll, country or a gospel tune.

**jerry scheff:** I think the reason he liked the band was that we listened to each other. We listened to him, and we instinctively picked up on what should be there. And me, not having any background in this music, I just listened to what everybody else was doing. I tried to pull out of my brain things that I'd heard in the past in that kind of music. At that time there hadn't been a lot of bass players that played that kind of music. The string bass had been done by Bill Black and those people, but that didn't translate to electric bass. So I had to make up what I thought should be there. If I were starting the whole thing now, the interesting thing is that I wouldn't do it the same way, 'cause I don't play that way anymore. I do it when I play these Elvis concerts. (Elvis Australia/www.elvis.com/au/Arjan Deelen)

**jerry schilling:** Elvis loved Jerry Scheff's bass playing. A lot of the R&B that we liked in the early '50s was bass driven. Think about "Bo Diddley. When Elvis introduced him he'd say, "Jerry Scheff with the thundering bass." I went to concerts with Elvis and he'd say, "Jerry, watch the bass player, he's always the coolest guy onstage." Don't forget that Elvis didn't even have a drummer early on. Bill Black was the whole rhythm on stand up bass. When you've played with Bill Black you know the importance of a bass player.

**john wilkinson:** Elvis had seen me on a couple of local Los Angeles TV shows and he liked the way I fingerpicked the guitar and the way I sang. Somehow he found my phone number. I'd done a lot of work around Los Angeles in studios and clubs. It was a Saturday afternoon and I was sitting at home in my house in North Hollywood and I was half drunk on red wine and watching old *Ozzie and Harriet* reruns on a black and white TV. A lot of my buddies knew that I was an Elvis fan since the first time I met him in 1954, '55 when I was nine years old. Sometimes my buddies would call me on the phone and try to sound like Elvis and make me think it was him on the phone. I picked up the phone, "Hello?" This voice comes on that sounded like Elvis. "Hey John, this is Elvis." I go, "Yeah, right!" Click. And I hung up. I thought, "Uh oh, that voice was awfully good, you don't suppose that I just hung up on Elvis Presley?" Almost immediately the phone rings again and I pick it up and I go, "Yes sir" and he goes, "Dammit Johnny, this is Elvis, don't hang up on me!" I said, "Elvis, I'm sorry" and explained what happened. He said, "Look, I'm putting a band together. We're gonna go back out on the road and I have one spot left for a rhythm guitar player. I think you'd be the one to fill it, would you like to have that job?" And I said, "Yeah, I would. I've only been a fan of yours since I was a little itty boy, I'd love to do it." He said, "I'll tell you what, I'm gonna have the other guys in the band up to the house

The Sweet Inspirations

tonight and we're gonna sit around and pick. Why don't you come on up? We'll see how things work and if we get along with one another."

So I hung up and not two minutes later the phone rings again and it's James Burton offering me the same job. I said, "Well James, Elvis just called me and offered me the job and I accepted it but I'll accept it from you too." (laughs) We got together and I knew all these guys because they'd played on my record when I was with RCA. It was just amazing working with those players; they're legends who worked with all the big name entertainers. They'd worked with (Frank) Sinatra, Emmylou Harris, you name it.

When we'd gotten together at the house Elvis started singing some of the old songs like "My Baby Left Me" and "Heartbreak Hotel." That night I told Elvis, "I'm a folk picker, I play acoustic guitar, I don't even own an electric guitar." He said, "Well, I'll tell you what…" And he wrote down a figure on a piece of paper. He said, "Here's what I propose to pay you per week." I looked at the figure and it was more money than I'd ever seen in my life. He said, "Now, are you an official rock and roll rhythm guitar?" and I said, "You bet your ass." (laughs) I was just thrilled to death to get the job.

**JAMES BURTON:** He got into the groove and worked real hard on the songs.

**LARRY MUHOBERAC:** John Wilkinson was a solid rhythm guitar player. We needed a really strong rhythm player to work alongside James Burton who took solos. Each person in the band just clicked.

> **RONNIE TUTT:** It was something about the energy. The difference in musical styles made it an interesting contrast. I don't know how to describe it, but it worked. (Elvis Australia/www.elvis.com/au/Arjan Deelen)

**MARTY LACKER:** George Klein and I were walking down the aisle with Elvis at the Memphian Theater and Elvis said, "I've got to think about finding some female backup singers for the shows in Vegas." He said he was gonna get the Blossoms but decided not to because they were backing Tom Jones in Vegas. So I said, "There's this new soul group called the Sweet Inspirations. You should check them out, they're great." I told him that Chips cut a hit on them with a song called "Sweet Inspiration." I said, "I think you'll like them because they're a combination of R&B and gospel." So I told him I'd bring him a copy to listen to. I went down to Graceland and brought him the "Sweet Inspiration" single and it knocked his ass out and that's how they got hired.

> **LISA MARIE PRESLEY:** I loved the song "Sweet Inspiration." I just loved their voices. They were like the Supremes then but they weren't as high profile. I think they were underrated because my father snagged them at some point.

**CISSY HOUSTON** (The Sweet Inspirations): The Sweet Inspirations worked with all kinds of artists, everyone from Carmen MacRae to Dusty Springfield. So it was no big thing for us to work with anybody and do what they want. But gospel was our first love. We came from church. Elvis's vocal style came from gospel. Even though he sang all kinds of music, gospel always flavored what he sang.

So it was the perfect fit to work with someone like Elvis.

> **MYRNA SMITH** (The Sweet Inspirations): Elvis wanted to have a black female group with a lot of soul and that's why he chose us. We were very happy to get the job.
>
> We met Elvis for the first time at our first rehearsal on the stage of the International Hotel. It was me, Cissy Houston, Estelle (Brown) and Sylvia (Shemwell). We were sitting on the stage and heard this rumbling and all of a sudden there was Elvis.

**ESTELLE BROWN** (The Sweet Inspirations): I was very nervous and afraid to meet Elvis. I didn't know what to expect.

> **MYRNA SMITH:** He showed up, introduced himself, "Hi, I'm Elvis" and gave each of us a kiss on the lips. Cissy was so excited she fell off her stool. (laughs) She was older than the rest of us and we didn't expect her to react like that but Elvis ignored it like it didn't happen.

**CISSY HOUSTON:** I was flabbergasted. Although I had the most handsome husband in the world Elvis looked wonderful. I looked at him and his eyes were so blue, it was unreal.

**myrna smith:** He was very charming. He had on a brown suit and had a deep tan. He was so gorgeous. He was everything you wanted in a man. You wouldn't believe how handsome he was unless you saw him in person. I fell in love with him as a person right at that moment. Listening to his music before that I knew he was a great singer but I didn't know the effect he would have on me when I met him.

**estelle brown:** The music we sang was completely different to the music he sang and I had no idea what could we possibly do to enhance his music. But as God would have it, everything worked out perfectly. It was a marriage made in heaven.

**myrna smith:** Before rehearsals Elvis's people sent a bunch of albums to New Jersey where we were all living at the time but we didn't listen to them. We were session singers and we learned quickly. We wanted to keep it fresh. So we just waited until we got to rehearsals before we learned the songs.

**cissy houston:** At first we weren't sure why we were asked to backup Elvis because we thought it was such a different kind of music. But when we started singing with him at rehearsals everything clicked. The sound blended so well. He and I really became good friends and we talked a lot.

**terry blackwood** (The Imperials): Elvis went to my home church, the First Assembly of God in Memphis, Tennessee because my family, the Blackwood Brothers Quartet, attended there. He was a big fan of gospel quartet music and his mother was a very devout Christian. Elvis had been following my family's career. He also loved the Statesmen with Jake Hess, another southern gospel group. He was also a big fan of the Harmonizing Four and several of the black gospel quartets. Because of his love for gospel music, when it came time for him to return to the stage in '69 he wanted a gospel quartet to back him up. Of course, he had his own reasons for wanting to use the Sweet Inspirations. They played a big part in contributing to his R&B sound. Elvis loved harmonies and he wanted to hear the bass voice and the three high male vocals because he grew up with that. It was just a natural extension of who he was.

**ray walker** (The Jordanaires): Elvis wanted the Jordanaires to back him in Vegas. When Elvis was planning to perform his first shows in Vegas, Tom Diskin called Gordon (Stoker) and asked us if we could go.

**gordon stoker** (The Jordanaires): I told Tom we'd have to get out of 40 sessions to do these five weeks in Vegas with him. There were only two groups in Nashville doing it at that time and that was the Anita Kerr Singers and the Jordanaires.

**ray walker:** We worked with artists that constantly held from number one through 25 on all the charts every month.

**gordon stoker:** I told Tom Diskin that I'd have to talk to the producers of these sessions. So I went to Chet Atkins and Owen Bradley, all these people that we were working for, and they said, "If you leave we'll have to get another group in town to do the background sessions because we've got to have a male quartet group."

**RAY WALKER:** They told Gordon that there was a possibility they'd keep using that group for sessions if the artist liked them.

**GORDON STOKER:** So we had to turn down the offer and we've always regretted it since.

**ELVIS PRESLEY:** Can't get them out of Nashville, man. They make so much money and they do so well in Nashville, you can't get them out of there. (Houston press conference, February 27, 1970)

**GORDON STOKER:** Elvis was very hurt at first but he later told me he understood. Had we gone to Vegas we would have lost a big Coca-Cola commercial, the one that goes (sings) "Coke is the real thing…" That was us. We made more money staying in Nashville and doing that commercial than we would have made the whole year working with Elvis. Because we were doing Elvis Presley's backgrounds, everyone else wanted us on their sessions. (laughs) Elvis opened a new world not only for us but D.J. (Fontana) and Scotty (Moore) in terms of session work. Elvis opened the doors for us to work with everyone from Patsy Cline to Rick Nelson and make a fat living doing sessions.

**RAY WALKER:** We'd done the *How Great Thou Art* album with Elvis in 1966. I suggested he do that song. We taught it to him and it became his signature song. The Imperials came in on that session along with Jake Hess and Millie Kirkham and several others. We knew the Imperials were a great group. We considered them the number one performing gospel quartet in the world. So Gordon suggested they use the Imperials.

**JOE MOSCHEO** (The Imperials): I called Gordon (Stoker) and asked what happened. They were asked before us, we were second choice. I think Gordon and the guys thought it was a one-time shot; they'd go to Vegas for a couple of weeks and at the end of that it was business as usual. They didn't know it would turn into a twice a year, 30 day engagement and last a long long time. To be a part of the final history of Elvis and his performances, I think if they had any foresight into that they would have said yes.

**TERRY BLACKWOOD:** At the time the Imperials were winning all the Grammy awards. He took note of us because he followed the Blackwood family and liked our songs a great deal. Elvis knew me from Memphis. I saw him occasionally at some of our gospel shows.

**JOE MOSCHEO:** The call came from Tom Diskin, who worked with Colonel Parker and was his right hand man. He asked about our availability for this four week run of shows. Of course we were very anxious to do it. We had worked with Elvis on records before August of '69— we appeared on all of the gospel albums. He loved our group and our sound and he liked us individually. Elvis was comfortable working with us.

**TERRY BLACKWOOD:** After we joined him in Las Vegas, whenever we were invited to the penthouse after our two shows a night we wouldn't sing rock and roll music. We'd sing gospel music around the piano. That's what he loved. He loved rock too but when he had four quartet around him he wanted to harmonize and sing the old black spirituals. That's the music he grew up hearing.

IMPACT
RECORDS

THE IMPERIALS

"Thanks For Voting Us no.1"

SUMAR TALENT AGENCY
912-17th AVE SO.
NASHVILLE, TENNESSEE
615- 255-8595

**elvis presley:** A lot of times we'll go upstairs and sing until daylight - gospel songs. We grew up with it.... It more or less puts your mind at ease. It does mine. (*Elvis on Tour*, 1972 interview)

**RONNIE TUTT:** No one had that kind of a band and singers the way he had it. He had a vision in a dream. He told me that. He told Colonel Parker that that's exactly what he wanted to do. The Colonel said, "No" because he wanted Elvis to go on there with dancing girls, like the '68 Special. But Elvis said, "I've had enough of those stupid movies. I don't want any more part of that. I just had this dream. I wanted a hard driving rhythm section, a rock 'n roll band, a big orchestra in the back, but no dancing, but all singing, with a black soul group and a white gospel group." So he called the Colonel up in the middle of the night, and said, "This is what I want to do." And the Colonel said, "No, no, no." Elvis said, "We're gonna do that, or I'm not going to Las Vegas" and he hung up. So he won. (laughs)
(Elvis Australia/www.elvis.com/au/Arjan Deelen)

# listen to the band

Inside Hollywood's RCA Studios, Elvis and band got down to business spending long hours perfecting their performance.

**john wilkinson:** Colonel Parker gave each one of us of a suitcase filled with every album Elvis had ever made. We took them home and listened to the records. Unbeknownst to Elvis we'd heard every song he ever recorded. So we had to be familiar with a lot of his songs. Elvis played a game that he called "Stump the band," where in the middle of a song he'd go, "I don't wanna do that song" and he'd turn around and say, "Let's do this" and he'd pull something out of the hat from way back.

**james burton:** He picked the songs that felt good to him. It was Elvis's call in terms of the songs he wanted to do but he always asked for our input. We learned the songs by either listening to the record or we'd have chord charts. He gave us all the freedom in the world to put our own stamp on the songs.

**john wilkinson:** Elvis didn't ask us to play the songs exactly like the records, he wanted us to play the songs the way we felt it. He wanted us to match his enthusiasm and his level of energy.

**ronnie tutt:** He'd say, "I don't care what we'd done before or what the other records are like," even his old standard records, whatever they are "I want us to do now, what we do now, I don't want us to try and imitate what we did back then." So the challenge was to play wide open and interpret the music, follow him and the excitement. (The Elvis Touch/July 2002)

**john wilkinson:** Sometimes we thought he'd start the songs off a bit too fast but it was his show and we went along with it.

**sonny west:** Even at rehearsals you could see how happy he was to be back. He was in great humor and doing crazy stuff. In rehearsals he wasn't worried about opening night. He was in the moment and having a great time, cutting up with the musicians. He seemed very relaxed, the same way he was on the Nashville sessions for the *Elvis is Back!* album, which was the first time I went to work for him.

**larry muhoberac:** Rehearsals were fun but pressurized. But things went smoothly. No hassles, no arguments. We were focusing on the music, refining it and getting the songs into shape. I could tell Elvis got a kick out of doing his early Sun songs like "Mystery Train." Everybody was behind him. We wanted it to work for him so badly.

**jerry scheff:** We went over a lot of songs, and then later we never rehearsed at all, so it's a good thing we rehearsed then! (laughs). But the saving grace was that Elvis never did anything the same way twice. We always had to keep our eye on him. You never could just, you know, relax (laughs). You had to pay attention. You never knew what he was gonna do. Never. (Elvis Australia/www.elvis.com/au/Arjan Deelen)

Elvis in rehearsals, MGM Studios,
Culver City, California, 1970

*(Author's note: no images have surfaced
of Elvis rehearsing with the band in 1969
hence we've reproduced this shot from
the following year to lend the feel of a
typical rehearsal)*

**lARRY muHoBERAC:** Elvis would ask, "Hey, do you know this or do you know that?" and he'd
play a little of it on guitar. Everybody already knew most of the songs and if someone didn't
remember how it went you'd pick it up by ear. Everybody had the kind of ear where they could
pick up songs quickly. They were used to playing a lot of styles. All the members of the band
were very versatile, which worked with the type of music Elvis was doing.

**SANdi miLLER** (fan): My friend Jan and I went to a lot of band rehearsals. They'd start at seven
or eight at night and go until two or three in the morning. Elvis would goof around a lot, make
jokes and sing everybody else's songs like Roy Orbison, Neil Sedaka, just whatever popped into
his head. If he wasn't in the mood to do what he was supposed to do he didn't do it. But you
could also tell he was a perfectionist. He'd do a song over and over again until it was right. In

rehearsals, he'd act as the conductor. He wasn't just standing there singing, he was in charge of everything. "Why don't you speed it up there?" or "that doesn't sound right, why don't we try it this way?" I remember him rehearsing "Memories". After about the third or fourth time through, he stopped and said, "Man, that's a pretty song."

**joe moscheo:** We're here in Nashville and so was Elvis's producer, Felton Jarvis. He worked at RCA Studios here in Nashville. He was his A&R guy and his producer. We were really good friends with Felton. Felton had put us on some sessions with Elvis and a lot of RCA sessions. Felton gave us a list of songs and recordings of Elvis. He said, "Learn these 30 to 50 songs and learn what the Jordanaires did and then put your own stamp on it. This is some of the stuff we'll be drawing from."

We rehearsed ourselves before we went out to Vegas. We were hired for four weeks starting the end of July and through August. We came in a week early for that rehearsal week. They brought the singers together first to work out our parts, when we sing and when we wouldn't sing with the girls. We were there in a ballroom at the International Hotel rehearsing with the Sweets while Elvis was working in California with the TCB band. He worked with them for a few weeks. Then it was time for Elvis and the band to show up and they came in. So it was the TCB band, the Sweet Inspirations, the Imperials and Elvis in that ballroom putting the show together.

**terry blackwood:** That involved at least eight hours of intense rehearsal a day.

**armond morales** (The Imperials): We'd keep going until he was tired. The show was still developing during that time. He had pretty much selected what he wanted to sing but he was test running it too in rehearsals.

**joe moscheo:** We worked about a week on that before we went to the stage in the showroom and worked with the big orchestra. You see a lot of it in *That's The Way It Is*, in his head Elvis knew exactly what he wanted. We never had to go very far to get an answer. He could hear it all. He was really in charge, especially with the arrangements.

**armond morales:** He never held back in rehearsals. He wore the carpet out with his feet and he was sweating with a towel around his neck when we rehearsed. He worked just as hard in rehearsals as he did when he gave a show. He wasn't holding back. He wanted to feel that intensity.

**joe moscheo:** He wore weights around his wrists and ankles. He was in training. He thought when he took the weights off he'd have a lot more energy and a lot more movement. He was 175 pounds and had a tan. He never looked better than that first year or two in Vegas.

**terry blackwood:** Elvis would go over a song four or five times until he got tired of it and then we'd go over another song four or five times. He already knew what he wanted. He would direct us and say, "Right here I want you to do this…" A lot of what he told us was what we'd been singing as southern gospel. He incorporated it into specific songs that would lend themselves to those kinds of harmonies. This pertains to the slow ballads, not the up-tempo songs.

**joe moscheo:** His idea of bringing in white gospel singers with black soul singers was really genius on his part because he covered the whole gamut of music. When the girls sang with us it gave us a lot of soul. But it also gave them a lot of range. It gave them better pitch, too. It was a better singing group when we were all together than when we were separate. It didn't take long for us to find that vocal mesh. At that time, we were in awe of the whole situation. We really respected the Sweets. They'd done backup work with Aretha (Franklin) and a lot of other people and had hits on their own. Cissy Houston was with them for the first gigs we did with Elvis. Some of the vocal parts that the Sweets put in on "Proud Mary" were really important to the overall sound. We wanted to hear them and certainly didn't want to get in their way. On the other hand they were very respectful of us and didn't want to get in our way.

**myrna smith:** Elvis gave us a lot of freedom. We'd sometimes put in parts that weren't on the record. He didn't give us much musical input except if he didn't like what we were doing. Then he'd wait until we had finished the song and tell us, "I don't want you to sing there." He did it in such a nice way where it wasn't like he was chastising us. We put our hearts into our work and every song was a challenge to us and we loved that.

**estelle brown:** We were a pop/rock group that had been brought up in the church and we always sang gospel anyway. So when we worked with the Imperials our vocal styles just gelled together. It makes no difference what you're singing because what comes from the heart reaches the heart.

**terry blackwood:** There were some songs that were a little bit more difficult to negotiate simply because some of the songs were of a style that we as a southern gospel group were not as familiar with. We were not really considered a southern gospel group; we were considered more of a contemporary gospel group. In a sense we employed harmonies like many of the southern gospel groups did but we approached the songs with harmonies and styles that were not so predictable. I think Elvis liked that a lot. On his gospel album, *He Touched Me*, he recorded five of our songs almost note for note to the way we recorded them on our *Love is the Thing* album.

**estelle brown:** We listened to Elvis sing in rehearsals and it gave us a better feel for what would work best in terms of vocal parts.

**myrna smith:** There were no problems with, "You're singing the wrong note" or "You're singing too loud." The sound was immaculate and we must have given him what he looking for because he was pleased.

**armond morales:** If he didn't like something you'd know it. I remember one time he called me out into the hallway after he told us all about something he didn't like. I thought he was gonna get on my case about something. He said, "I really scared the hell out of them, didn't I?" and then he laughed

**joe moscheo:** When we were working out the vocal parts, and if you listen to the music, the vocal licks are part of the hook, just like some of the bass lines that Jerry Scheff did or some of the guitar licks that James Burton did. Elvis knew he needed a great performing band. He knew he needed a show drummer that had the stamina to drive the band. Ronnie brought so much energy as a drummer. When you back Elvis you lose five pounds a night just following the guy around the stage. He really drove the performance.

**TERRY blAckwood:** We did a lot of songs in the rehearsals that never made it to the stage in Las Vegas because either he decided it wasn't happening, didn't like the way it sounded or didn't think he could convey that song as effectively as he thought he could and he'd drop it.

**joe moscheo:** We knew 50 songs so if at any moment he'd throw in something different we were ready for it.

**bobby morris** (orchestra leader, Bobby Morris Orchestra): Prior to working with Elvis I worked with Frank Sinatra, Nat King Cole, Bobby Darin, Louis Prima, and Eddie Fisher. Since 1967, I was involved with Bill Miller who was the entertainment director at the Flamingo Hotel. The International Hotel was being built at the time and I was booking acts for Bill at the Flamingo. I asked him who he had coming in and he said, "Well, Barbra Streisand, Elvis Presley, Pearl Bailey and Bill Cosby, a whole bunch of people." He said, "Would you be interested in being the musical director for the lounge?" I said, "Well, who do you do have coming in there?" And he said, "People like Peggy Lee, Frankie Laine, and the Mills Brothers." I said, "Fine, I'll handle that. Who's gonna be in the big room?" He told me Harry James would be the conductor. A month before the opening of the International Bill called me and said, "Harry James reneged, would you like to be the musical conductor in the big showroom in the International?" I said, "Okay." I hadn't been a conductor before but I played drums and percussion and write music. A drummer is basically a conductor with a band. He sets the tempo. I took a conducting course with Keith Moon, a musical professor at the University of Nevada-Las Vegas and I had to learn it quickly.

I worked with Barbra Streisand for four weeks for the opening of the showroom and I knew Elvis was coming in next. I get a call from Bill Miller who says Colonel Parker wants to meet you. I met with him and he said, "I know you're the musical director for the hotel but we also want you to be a conductor for Elvis and we'll pay you." They flew me to Hollywood and we took a limo up to Elvis's house in the Hollywood Hills. I stayed with him for a few weeks listening to tunes and picking out the material that I thought would work best. We listened to hundreds of recordings. Every time I would get excited he would get excited. He was very knowledgeable musically and had a natural feel and knew exactly what he wanted.

Elvis was not a rock and roller anymore. He was changing gears and going into nightclubs, which was a completely different thing. "Memories" and all those other beautiful tunes required strings. We did some rock tunes, of course, but Elvis was now becoming a more well-rounded entertainer and versatile singer.

My function was to incorporate all the songs with an orchestra. For those Vegas shows, we had a big orchestra, which consisted of 20, 25 strings, violas, cellos, violins. We had a brass section, saxes, trumpets, trombones. We also had percussion players too.

**loAnne miller pArker:** They were top notch musicians. Many of them played with big groups and they got tired of the road. Playing in Vegas gave them a home life.

**joe moscheo:** He could have done without the orchestra. On certain songs the orchestral instrumentation was also a hook--"American Trilogy" has a flute solo and "The Wonder of You" has a bass trombone lick that he loved and would always turn around to hear. But in a live environment it's hard to mix an orchestra with a band and allow it all to be heard clearly. I don't think the mix was ever good enough where it enhanced anything.

**estelle brown:** Even though he was a superstar he didn't act like a superstar with us. He was a down to earth, loving guy. We loved working with Elvis. Whoever was working with him, whether it was the TCB band, the Sweet Inspirations or the Imperials, we all had to be family. Elvis was so loving toward all of us. He didn't try to present himself as being above anybody else. He was just a human being like you or I. Because he stayed grounded it kept him pure.

**terry blackwood:** There are so many Elvis impersonators who go out and try to be Elvis and they're so cocky and so self assured. They think the whole world revolves around them. Elvis never acted like he was some big star and that we were lucky to be working with him. I felt he was a man who wanted to do his best but was never really sure if the fans would embrace him. He needed friends and associates to tell him, "You're gonna do great! Don't worry about it." He wasn't really sure he was such a great star. Deep down I think Elvis was very insecure and very shy. He needed constant reinforcement by the Memphis Mafia that he was great and that people were gonna love him. He was nervous about the Vegas shows. Had I been him I would have been nervous too. He had to go out there and prove that he was the king of rock and roll, that he was as good as everybody thought he was.

**armond morales:** Elvis was definitely under some pressure. He was against a timeline and needed to be ready for that first opening show. He was excited about being in front of a live audience again but you could sense his apprehension too. He wanted to do well and didn't want to let down his fans. Everybody had to reassure him that he was gonna be fabulous.

**loanne miller parker:** At the beginning, Colonel wasn't totally confident that Elvis's return to performing would be a major success. It was an experiment for both of them. He hadn't played live in eight years and a lot changes in that amount of time.

**nicholas naff:** Elvis wasn't a proven Las Vegas act. There was some worry that perhaps Elvis would not be able to make the transition as a Las Vegas act. But he proved everyone wrong. Colonel Parker had a good notion of what Elvis would do in terms of business and he never failed to remind us of that. (laughs) It became apparent immediately that Elvis's first engagement at the International would be a great success.

**colonel tom parker:** Elvis has worked extremely hard for his show. But then he is one of the most dedicated entertainers I have ever been associated with. (*Billboard*, August 9, 1969/ James D. Kingsly)

**joe esposito:** After the rehearsals in Hollywood, we went to Vegas and rehearsed at the hotel for another week before the opening night.

**priscilla presley:** Elvis didn't let me come to rehearsals. He was very much into his own world at that time. He wanted to surprise everyone. He was also very nervous. He didn't want anyone to take him out of those moments.

# dressed to thrill

Bill Belew, who designed Elvis's costumes for the '68 special, was tapped to create something special for The King's '69 shows in Las Vegas.

**bill belew** (Elvis's costume designer): When I started out designing for Elvis when he first appeared in Las Vegas, the only thing that came to mind was that I didn't want him to be the typical Las Vegas show person. So I sculpted the clothes so that they enhanced his performance. I didn't want him to be a 'Liberace type person' so I started out simple and we built on that. (Interview conducted by Julie Mundy for *Elvis Fashion - From Memphis to Graceland*)

**SONNY WEST:** In 1956, Elvis played the New Frontier Hotel, and his audience was too young to come there so they bought out his contract. During that time he met Liberace. Liberace wore these flamboyant outfits and Elvis said, "Man, you're out there, that costume is something." He told Elvis, "Well, if anything ever happens and I lose my voice or break a finger and can't play piano I can always put on a fashion show." (laughs) That stayed with him. You've gotta remember that Elvis dressed different even in high school; he wore the pinks and the blacks that they were wearing in other cities like New York. So the costumes he started wearing during that first engagement in Vegas and for the rest of his career like the jumpsuits, big belts and the capes came from his own sense of style and Liberace's showmanship and wardrobe.

**bill belew:** He had a terrific build at that point . . . [But] at the time we started in Vegas, everything was Liberace. And I would see these outlandish things with fur and feathers and think, "That's not going to be Elvis. And if that's what he wants, he can get somebody else." I wanted the clothes to be easy and seductive and that was it. And I never wanted anything to compromise his masculinity. (*Salon*)

What we wanted to do at the time was experiment as to what would be the best look for him. And, of course, that was really my first time working in Vegas. Having worked on the stage in New York it's quite different. But the lighting there was still in its early stages. And we found that the color that worked the best was white. It allowed them to change the colors on him, whereas black would absorb all the color. And it was hard to highlight him. And we experimented with blue which was one of his favorite colors. Red. But it just ended up that white was the best thing and, of course, you know, you want the star to be the person, and not the wardrobe. I've always been very lucky in that, as I say now, when I talk to the fan clubs. Bob Mackie had Cher, I had Elvis Presley. I mean, it was a fabulous body to design for. He really wore and had a flair for clothes. When we went to Vegas, I contacted Ice Capades, and I talked to some friends of mine there. And I said, "Would ya'll be interested in making Elvis Presley's clothes for Vegas?" Because I would like to use what is known by ice skaters as stretch gab, or gabardine. And, it allows skaters to do their splits, their turns, and everything. And I thought it would be great for Elvis because the one thing he said that he wanted to incorporate in his act was karate. And I thought I've got to find something that will allow him to do that. (Elvis Australia/www.elvis.com/au/Arjan Deelen)

**INTERNATIONAL**

Thank you...

     ...for your early interest in the new and exciting Las Vegas International Hotel.

     We are pleased to announce formal Grand Opening Ceremonies have been scheduled for July 2 and 3, 1969. Reservations are now being accepted for guest accommodations after July 6.

     In addition, Miss Barbra Streisand will perform twice nightly in the Showroom Internationale at 8:00 p.m. and at midnight through July 30.

     Elvis Presley is scheduled from July 31 through August 28.

     To assist you in making room reservations, we are enclosing a postage paid request card. Simply fill out the accommodations desired and drop in the mail.

     For Showroom reservations only, please direct your request to: Maitre D', Showroom Internationale, International Hotel, Las Vegas, Nevada.

     Also enclosed is a descriptive brochure to further acquaint you with the unique facilities and services that await you at the Las Vegas International Hotel.

     Again, thank you for your interest in our new resort. We look forward to welcoming you into International Territory in the very near future.

              Most Cordially,

              MICHAEL LINDECK
              Manager

ML:j
Enclosures (2)

# hype, publicity and promotion

A master of publicity and promotion, the Colonel, in tandem with the International Hotel, would construct a massive promotional campaign championing The King's long-awaited return to the stage.

**colonel tom parker:** This town has never seen a promoter like me. (Interview by Earl Wilson, *Lima News*, August 7, 1969)

**bruce banke:** The hotel's publicity department was completely unprepared for the onslaught from the hundreds of writers who wanted to cover Elvis's return to live performing. The phones had been ringing all month with requests for press seating for opening night. Calls came in from Europe, Japan, Australia, Great Britain and from every major entertainment writer in the United States. Kerkorian made his private DC-9 available to fly in key writers from New York, Chicago and the Southern California area. They eventually had to spread the press out over the next few nights to accommodate them all.

**t.g. sheppard** (then known as Bill Browder, head of Southeast regional promotion, RCA Records): There was an astronomical demand from press to cover the opening show. There were no cameras or video allowed into the showroom so when the press got there they tried to talk to someone inside the organization like Joe Esposito to give them the inside story.

**rona barrett** (gossip columnist): There was a lot of hype about Elvis's comeback in '69. The PR on that was so extraordinary and Las Vegas joined in on the hype. The press were excited and columnists all over the country were interested in knowing how fat or thin he was, what he looked like, and what he was going to wear. Sometimes there can be a backlash to that hype. But remember, no matter what the press may say, it's really the public that makes the difference. If they were pleased and happy, word of mouth would spread. "You've got to go and see Elvis at the International!" I think every human being has their own thermometer. And when that thermometer goes off it's hard to keep it down.

**bob finkel** (executive producer, *Singer Presents Elvis*): After doing the TV special Elvis gained a lot more fans. Many of them had never seen him perform before. Those people who saw the special now wanted to see him onstage in Las Vegas.

**bruce banke:** Fans from around the world were tying up hotel phone lines requesting show and room reservations. The entire engagement was almost sold out before it started. Las Vegas had never seen an opening like it before and likely never will again. One indicator that Las Vegas was at a fever pitch in late July is the fact the southern Nevada area set an all-time high temperature record of 113 degrees.

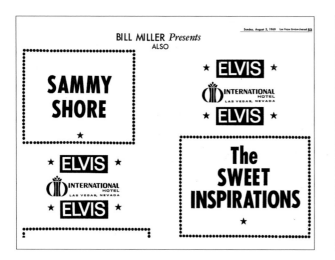

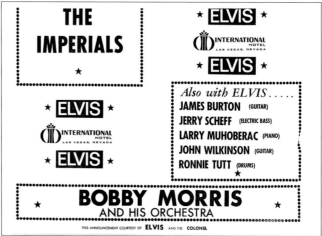

**nicholas naff:** Colonel practically lived in my offices. He was there all the time. He had good publicity ideas and was our advisor on how to publicize Elvis. His ideas were perfect for him. He really knew his client well. How we publicized Elvis's first live performances wasn't much different than how we worked with other acts. The publicity strategies that we employed weren't that much different but the scope of them was. The hotel naturally was willing to spend a lot of money to publicize his shows.

**joe esposito:** Colonel felt very comfortable about the deal and that Elvis could pull it off. He told him, "Elvis, I'll let people know you're in this town but you're gonna be the one who brings them in."

**loanne miller parker:** Colonel didn't miss a trick. Remember, he's an ex-carny and they know how to flaunt it. (laughs) He did everything he could to ensure that everybody knew Elvis would be in town playing the International. Information went out to all the fan clubs. The International Hotel put out some of their own advertising. Nick Naff and later Bruce Banke, who would handle publicity for the hotel, followed the Colonel's instructions. You'd see taxi cabs with signs on top about Elvis's show. You'd see benches at bus stops and the backs of the benches would have Elvis's name on them.

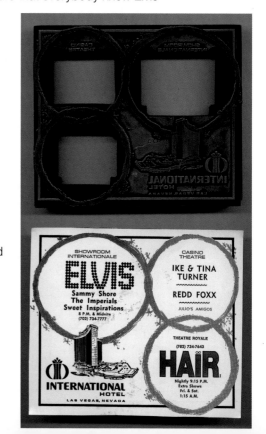

**nicholas naff:** We began to put up billboards for Elvis's show a day or two before his opening. Of course, they would increase in density on opening day. If you were a Barbra Streisand you didn't want another act to have billboards all over the place while you were still performing during your run. We also couldn't distribute any promotional material throughout the hotel until Elvis's show opened. You didn't do that because that would be offensive to the artist that was appearing there.

**alex shoofey:** The campaign that he (the Colonel) produced was unbelievable. He had every billboard in the entire city, not only in Vegas, but leading all the way to California. (Mr. Rock & Roll documentary, 1999)

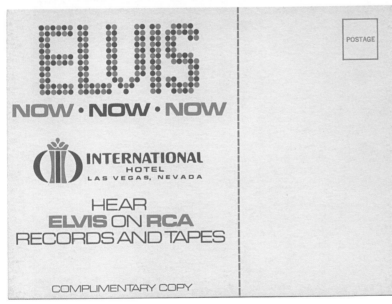

*Greetings from Las Vegas*      *International Hotel*

**alex shoofey:** The Colonel was a remarkable individual. He said, "I just want one word on your billboard, Elvis. That's all, nothing else." (UNLV Oral History Research Center, March 2003)

**loanne miller parker:** Before Elvis it was quite unusual for entertainers to have more than one or two billboards in Las Vegas. But Colonel put them everywhere. After that, all the stars would want the same promotional treatment. They'd say, "If Elvis has it, I want it too!"

**joe esposito:** The minute you landed in Vegas, you knew Elvis was in town.

**carol kaye** (concert attendee): I arrived at the airport and there were slot machines and posters of Elvis plastered all over. It was like you were walking into Elvis's house. Then we drove onto the strip and there were huge billboards everywhere with big letters that said, "ELVIS PRESLEY

# Elvis, Now Thru August 28!

The New
International Hotel

IN PERSON AT THE INTERNATIONAL HOTEL!" It was Elvis's town. I couldn't breathe, I was crying, I was laughing, I was so excited. I felt like the luckiest person in the world.

**joe esposito:** There were also tons of radio and TV commercials that just covered the city and let everybody know that Elvis would be playing the International.

**nicholas naff:** I wrote all the radio commercials. They were 60-second commercials and naturally we sent them to radio stations everywhere, Las Vegas, California. One of the spots we ran only used one word throughout the commercial, "ELVIS! ELVIS! ELVIS!" The Colonel favored that approach. The other commercials I wrote had more copy telling people how great his show was and were more sales oriented.

**bobby vinton:** I remember having lunch with Colonel Parker the afternoon of Elvis's first show. I asked the Colonel if he'd take me on as a client. He said, "No no, I won't handle anybody but Elvis." While I'm sitting there talking to him he's on the phone calling up all the radio stations and he's saying, "Are there any spots available? I want every available spot." He wanted every available radio spot to say that Elvis was opening at the International. I looked at him and said, "Why are you doing this now? Elvis is already sold out and you can't get in. There are lines of people screaming to get in and you're screaming to buy more spots." And he said, "That's why he sold out." I asked him, "Who's gonna pay for all these spots?" and he said, "I'm gonna send the bill to the record company, let them pay for it." So I learned a lot from that luncheon with the Colonel about the way he and Elvis operated.

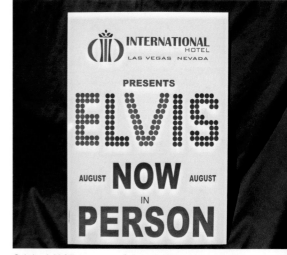

Original 1969 press conference placard

**nicholas naff:** The Colonel had a really good feel of how to market Elvis. He knew how to get the most for his artist. He reminded me of that famous circus guy, Barnum. That was his whole career. That's all he did. He took that circus background and applied principles of that to Elvis's career in terms of promotion and publicity.

**loanne miller parker:** August was the hottest month for a performer to appear. During the seasonal holidays like Thanksgiving and Christmas, Las Vegas was a ghost town. Mainly people came during the summer months when they were on vacation or school was out. Elvis would return to Las Vegas to perform twice a year both in January and in August. A lot of the high rollers would call and say, "When is Elvis coming back?" Their wives were at every show and their husbands were thrilled because they could be out in the casino gambling.

**t.g. sheppard:** RCA knew there was a whole new movement of Elvis fans that were coming along. We felt it in sales and all of our media outlets, which we closely monitored. Elvis's return to live performances was a way to get that audience.

# OPENING ACTS

Elvis's backing group, the Sweet Inspirations and veteran comedian Sammy Shore were slated to open the show.

**SAMMY SHORE** (comedian): I was working at the Riviera Hotel and I was a big hit. Bill Miller, the entertainment head of the Flamingo Hotel and the International Hotel, wanted me to come to the Flamingo and work with Tom Jones who was very hot at the time. So I went in and worked with Tom and I was a hit over there. One night Elvis and the Colonel came in and saw me. They came backstage with Bill Miller and Elvis said, (imitates Elvis), "Sammy, you're a real funny guy, I'd like you to come and open for me at the International Hotel." I couldn't believe it. He liked my sense of humor. Sometimes Elvis would stand on the side of the stage and watch my act and he would laugh at me. That's the name of my new book, *The Man Who Made Elvis Laugh*. As for my act, I was told, "Just do 25 minutes." No one had to tell me to be clean because I always worked clean. I never even used the word 'shit' in my act.

# THE MAIN EVENT

Dateline: July 31, 1969. Inside the International Hotel there was a bustle of activity and palpable excitement as fans, press, VIPs and dignitaries gathered to witness Elvis's first live show in many years.

**bruce banke:** Early in the morning of July 31, with the temperature already over 100 degrees, Ad Art Sign Company crews began lifting huge 10-foot high ELVIS letters, designed by the Colonel, into place on both faces of the mammoth International marquee in front of the hotel. They were so large they went up in 16 separate pieces and had to be wired down instead of clipped on like normal letters. The letters were larger than any used on a Las Vegas marquee in the past and workers were worried that they would blow off and injure someone if they weren't tied down.

**bill medley** (The Righteous Brothers): When Elvis came to town, it was the first time Las Vegas was rock and roll. It was a rock and roll casino and that was the first ever.

**emilio muscelli:** Every room in the hotel was sold out and the casino was packed.

**t.g. sheppard:** There were people that would have paid anything to get into those shows.

**terry blackwood:** The vibe inside the hotel was electrifying, especially the first night. And this went on for months on end.

**chris hutchins:** The place was buzzing. The guards were throwing people out, front and center.

**terry blackwood:** You had all this press and hoopla about Elvis's return to live performances. All these fans that had never seen him before came to the shows.

**bruce banke:** At this time, the Colonel established a tradition that would become his standard operating procedure for the next seven years. As soon as the audience was seated for Barbra's final midnight performance, he turned the hotel into an Elvis fantasy land. Custom-made banners, pennants, posters, over-sized cardboard records, and pictures were plastered on every pillar and wall, both inside and outside the hotel.

**joe moscheo:** It was like an Elvis retail store.

Elvis souvenir stand, International Hotel, 1971

**terry blackwood:** It looked like a political convention, like "Elvis for President."

**sammy shore:** It was like walking into a carnival. Colonel Parker promoted Elvis like he did when he worked in the circus.

**t.g. sheppard:** RCA produced many promotional items for the shows like banners and key chains and these items were given away as souvenirs to people when they'd leave.

**joe esposito:** Waitresses would be wearing Elvis buttons. It made it very exciting. The other casinos loved it too because he brought them a lot of business as well.

**JOE MOSCHEO:** The Colonel made sure that every dealer in the casino wore a straw hat with Elvis's name on it. They also wore red, white and blue arm bands with Elvis's name on it too.

**JIMMY NEWMAN** (executive vice-president of casino operations, International Hotel): It was aggravating to the dealers to have to wear those straw hats and arm bands. It was a distraction for them. That was a carny thing and we were an upscale gaming joint. But to the Colonel's credit, it worked to build excitement.

**JERRY SCHILLING:** Late one night after one of his shows Elvis said, "Let's just walk through the casino" and we did. We're walking through there and he saw the blackjack dealers wearing those straw hats with the word "ELVIS" on them—that was the first time he'd ever seen them—and he threw his hands up in the air and went, "Hey guys, it's not my fault" And everybody laughed.

**TERRY BLACKWOOD:** There was nothing subtle about Elvis's debut. It was all blatant in your face promotion, which was the Colonel's strength. That's how he made his living before he started working with Elvis and that played over into the Elvis world.

**STEVE BINDER:** The Colonel brought carny to show business. Promotion and marketing was his whole thing. There were posters everywhere of Elvis. It was just that kind of subliminal brain washing.

**JIMMY NEWMAN:** Colonel was always one jump ahead of everyone.

**GEORGE HAMILTON:** Colonel was a showman that knew the pulse of the people before they did.

**FRANK LIEBERMAN** (staff writer, *Los Angeles Herald-Examiner*): Some laughed at the circus-like atmosphere. I think there was a side of the public that thought it hurt his image. They thought it took away from the seriousness of his performance. They felt Colonel Parker had to create a carnival atmosphere because maybe Elvis wasn't that great a performer

**STEVE BINDER:** Look at where this country's gone in terms of politics and promotion and advertising and all that stuff. The Colonel was just ahead of the curve when it came to promoting an artist. But creativity was the last thing on the Colonel's mind.

**BOBBY VINTON:** I was performing at the Flamingo Hotel and you weren't allowed to put up banners or anything. I walked into the International and there were banners, pennants and teddy bears everywhere saying "ELVIS!" (laughs) I tried to do that kind of stuff at the Flamingo Hotel and they said, "This is sophisticated here, we don't want pennants that will make it look like a circus." The Colonel was so powerful, he could say, "That's what I want and that's what I get." The rules changed with Elvis and the Colonel.

**CHRIS HUTCHINS:** That night the Colonel wore a long white coat with stuff promoting Elvis. He was the merchandise man that night; before the show he was out front selling programs.

THE COLONEL SAYS "HOW MUCH DOES IT COST IF IT'S FREE"

**LOANNE MILLER PARKER:** The Elvis souvenirs were sold at a couple of tables set up right inside of the hotel. The proceeds from those went to a different charity each time. They'd sell small teddy bears, posters, photo albums and record albums.

**chris hutchins:** Parker loved doing the hype. When I first met Parker back in '64 he told me he was gonna write his life story and he was gonna call it, *"How Much Does It Cost If It's Free?"* It never occurred to me at that stage except that I had the scoop of the title of Colonel Parker's book. But it never mentioned Elvis, it never mentioned show business. Parker was talking about money and deals and he was more interested in that than anything else. I went to Parker's homes in Los Angeles and Vegas and I never saw a record player. I don't think he listened to the music; he wasn't particularly interested. I did ask him how involved he got with Elvis's music and he said that he stayed out of it except for the time that had asked Elvis to record "Are You Lonesome Tonight?"

**bruce banke:** Every night the fans would tear down anything they could reach and the next morning the Colonel would have it all replaced. The Colonel would say, "It's the best kind of advertising we could possibly do." At the conclusion of every four-week engagement the fans were encouraged to take down everything. By the next morning, the only things remaining that would indicate an Elvis appearance had just concluded were a few pieces of Scotch tape on the walls and a couple of dangling strings. It was like a hoard of locusts had gone through.

**joe moscheo:** We weren't used to the Vegas world. We were based out of Nashville. We sang at some gospel concerts and in churches. Our world and universe was so much smaller than that Las Vegas environment.

**bill miller:** The closing night of Barbra (Streisand) we had a big party. At five or six in the morning, my wife and I went to bed. We went downstairs and the lobby was jam-packed. They were standing three blocks away to get in to see Elvis that night. (*Las Vegas Desert Sun*, May 3, 1998)

**jimmy newman:** The showroom was located in the far end of the casino. Fans started lining up at ten o'clock in the morning for an eight o'clock show.

The lines for the show went all the way through the casino and out the front door.

**joe moscheo:** I think they did it on purpose so people could go, "Wow, this is the line to Elvis's show."

**maria columbus** (concert attendee): My friend, Jeannie and I waited around while people were filing into the showroom for the opening show. We didn't have reservations for that show because it was invitation only. We were going the next night, which was the first show open to the public. The showroom host, Jerry Baum was letting all the celebrities go by inside of a velvet rope. Our heads were swinging back and forth watching all the big name celebrities walk in. 15 to 20 minutes later Jerry came over and said, "An extra booth opened up, do you want to come in and see the show?" We thought he was joking until we realized he was serious. We ended up in the first row of booths for Elvis's opening performance.

**loanne miller parker:** It had been so long since people had seen Elvis live. They'd seen him in movies and on TV and the '68 television special brought him even closer to his fans. The '69 shows in Las Vegas was a further extension of the '68 special. The fans were salivating to see him in person.

**terry blackwood:** You'd be dressed up, you'd sit at a table, you'd have a nice tablecloth covered dinner and then you'd have the show. A lot of people were seeing him for the first time ever. They'd traveled in from around the world. Then you had some fans who would go to 20, 30, 40 shows. And of course the maître d' got rich. If you tipped the maître d' enough you could get down front. A lot of people were tipping heavily to get down to the front tables.

**loanne miller parker:** The captain would walk people to the assigned seats that Emilio gave them. Quite often if the seats were terrible money changed hands again and the captain said, "Oh wait a minute, I think I can find something a little closer."

**joe moscheo:** Emilio, the head maître d' raked it in.

**armond morales:** He bought a home and few cars. He was very fortunate. He was at the right place at the right time.

**marty lacker:** Emilio ingratiated himself with Elvis right away because of his personality. He was always up, smiling and laughing. He would come back to the dressing room after each show and tell us how everything went and you'd look at him and see that his both of his pants pockets were bulging with the tips he'd received. After a while we'd ask him, "Well Emilio, how'd you do tonight?" and he'd just pat that pocket and smile. (laughs) You gotta remember, especially in the earlier years, a lot of high rollers wanted to see Elvis's show and even though they were comped with free tickets they'd always leave a nice tip 'cause they wanted good seats— a hundred dollar bill here, a hundred dollar bill there. I'd imagine Emilio was making a couple of thousand a night in tips.

**lou toomin:** He became a millionaire from Elvis Presley's seven-year run engagement at the International. Those tips really added up. (laughs)

# all that glitters is gold

The setting for Elvis's comeback was the largest showroom in Vegas.

**bruce banke:** One of the key features at the International Hotel was its main showroom. It was the largest room of its kind in the world and it featured the finest light and sound system possible. The mammoth stage was 60-feet wide and over 200-feet deep and was designed to handle both superstars and major production shows. Even the doors leading into the huge dressing rooms in the basement were 10-feet high to permit showgirls through with their large feathered head pieces.

**emilio muscelli:** I helped design the showroom with the architect Maury Mason and his son, Stu.

**millie kirkham** (background soprano vocalist): The showroom was gorgeous and was very elegant at that time with its crystal chandeliers.

**terry blackwood:** There were angel figurines on the walls. To me it was a little bit gaudy.

**don short** (music writer, *The Daily Mirror*): It was tacky and larger than life but that's what Vegas is really like. You don't go to Vegas if you don't expect having that kind of thing blinding you like headlights.

**emilio muscelli:** Show business at that time changed with names like Elvis Presley and Barbra Streisand. Their attraction was enormous so we built the biggest showroom in the world. The showroom at the Flamingo only held about 700 people, the showroom in the International held 2000 people.

...and the world's **GREATEST ENTERTAINMENT** ... more than you ever dreamed...all on International Territory!

And the sound system is incredible. Something you won't believe. ♣ So the show scene really reigns at the International, like nowhere else in the world. In its big showroom ...in the legitimate theatre...and in its colorful show lounge, where the star attractions go on from late afternoon till early in the morn.

But you don't sit back and just watch others in International Territory. You can get into the act yourself. In our gaming casino. The largest ever built under one roof. Where we've got blackjack, roulette, pan, baccarat, keno and slot machines. In a glittering atmosphere that's as exciting as any you've ever experienced.

The International, suddenly, raises Las Vegas entertainment to new heights. Theatre, yes. But also the greatest names in the show world. Not only from Hollywood, TV and Broadway, but from London, Paris and other capitals of the world. ♣ Barbra Streisand opens the hotel. Followed by Elvis Presley and a stream of magnificent stars. And they're on display in America's truly great showroom. Not just for size (2,000 seats), but mostly for its beauty, comfort, luxury--and superb service out of not one, but two, modern kitchens, each from a different side of the room.

### FILLER ITEMS

The stage of the Showroom Internationale at the new Las Vegas International Hotel is the largest of its kind in the world, even bigger than Radio City Music Hall's in New York. Still, the design of the 2,000-seat showroom is such that a solo performer can be given intimate and personal staging.

\# \# \#

At 30 stories and 365 feet, the new International Hotel is the tallest building in Las Vegas. Only Hoover Dam and the Nevada Test Site, both government projects, exceed the International's $60 million cost and over-all dimensions in Nevada.

\# \# \#

The new International Hotel ordered all its chandelier crystal from Czechoslovakia. The order was the largest ever shipped from that country to the U.S.A.

\# \# \#

With 1,519 rooms, the new International Hotel in Las Vegas becomes the largest resort hotel in the world. Another 1,500 rooms have already been designed for adding to the hotel within the next 18 months.

\# \# \#

more...

Artist rendering of showroom

**TERRY blackwood:** It dwarfed every other hotel showroom in town.

**joe moscheo:** When we saw the showroom for the first time, we were struck by the size of it, it was unbelievable. It's nothing compared to what we have now, but back then in '69 it was huge.

**TERRY blackwood:** The fact that it was the biggest room in town is probably why Colonel Parker and Elvis went there. They knew they could pack it. It was the only showroom at that time which had a balcony.

**joe esposito:** The people with the International Hotel thought it was too big and wondered if he could fill it night after night. I could tell Elvis was even a little bit nervous about that.

**emilio muscelli:** Elvis's shows were first announced to the public four months before he played at the hotel.

**alex shoofey:** We got calls from all over the world. We couldn't accept all the reservations. (Mr. Rock & Roll documentary, 1999)

**emilio muscelli:** We sold out the whole four week engagement in five days. An enormous amount of people came to see him from all over the world.

**colonel tom parker:** Elvis has sold it out so far and each show has been capacity, which makes us very happy. (*Melody Maker*/August 23, 1969/Tony Wilson) (Author's note: Performing 58 sold out shows, 130,157 people attended Elvis's four week engagement with profits totaling $1,522, 635)

**terry blackwood:** The showroom was always packed. It had a huge stage, which was big enough to hold a 40-piece orchestra.

**emilio muscelli:** I was in charge of the whole showroom, reservations, end service, attendance and seating. The 8 P.M. show seated less people because we were serving dinner. The second show was held at midnight and the seating was much larger. With the first show you got dinner and a show and the second two drinks were included in the price of the show. We were seating an average of 4000 people a night.

**loanne miller parker:** It was $15 dollars to get in. For the dinner show price of $15 you would get the show and your choice of prime rib, a New York steak, lobster tail or capon. Drinks were extra and there was also a wine list that was extra too. For the midnight show, you paid $15 for the show and two drinks.

**chris hutchins:** I think Elvis was hurt that Parker made the hotel reduce the ticket price dramatically because Parker didn't think Elvis fans would pay anything like what they'd paid to see Frank Sinatra or Tom Jones. It bothered Elvis that Parker underestimated his value.

**loanne miller parker:** The Colonel wanted to keep ticket prices as low as possible and the hotel wanted the ticket prices to be higher.

**george hamilton:** His real audience didn't have the money to see him in a Vegas showroom so The Colonel said, "Listen, you've got to change the ticket price of people coming in here. These are people coming from Tupelo and Memphis and they want to see Elvis, you can't charge these prices."

**loanne miller parker:** He said, "most of our fans are gonna have to sacrifice to come to Las Vegas and also pay the money to see the show." Over the years the hotel did increase the prices and the Colonel was very unhappy about it. And the fans who wanted the really good seats had to pay even more money because of the tipping. The tipping policy upset the Colonel a lot but it was a Las Vegas tradition that he couldn't change.

MINIMUM CHARGE
$15
PER PERSON

**loanne miller parker:** Right below the stage there were tables that were perpendicular to the stage. The chairs were very very close. Of course, they seated as many people as possible at each table. Then behind those tables there was King's row. That was a row of booths that were red velvet and very ornate. They were reserved for the big high rollers and VIP's. Behind that was Queen's row. Behind those booths, the tables were placed horizontals to the stage. Then behind that was another row of booths and then there were tables the rest of the way up. There was a balcony above and it was all tables. Elvis had three of the center booths in King's row and Colonel had three of the center booths in Queen's row. They were all reserved for friends and family. One of the rules we had was every afternoon by five o'clock—this was when I worked in Colonel's office—I would call downstairs to showroom reservations and say, "The Colonel will not be using his booth or he will be using booth one and two."

Showroom **Internationale**

*Elvis*

*Appetizers*
Seafood Cocktail Supreme • Neptune 1.50,
Supreme of Fresh Fruit au Kirsch 1.00
Fresh Chopped Chicken Livers 1.00

*Salad*
Hearts of Romaine with Crab Meat
Choice of Dressing

*Entrees*
Baked Lobster Tail • Internationale 15.00
Breast of Young Capon, Souvaroff, Wild Rice 15.00
Roast Prime Rib of Beef, au Jus 15.00
Broiled New York Steak, Maitre d'Hotel 15.00
Broiled Tomato          Parisienne Potatoes

*Desserts*
Savarin Glacé Napoleon 1.00   Parfait Internationale 1.00
Fresh Strawberry Tart, Chantilly 1.00
Assorted Ice Creams and Sherbet .75

**bobby morris:** The sound in the showroom was impeccable. It was first class all around; you had all the best sound and light people.

**emilio muscelli:** Elvis was enormously popular but he had a different kind of clientele than Barbra Streisand. She had a more traditional clientele like a Sinatra while Elvis's audience was a more rock and roll crowd.

**loanne miller parker:** Back in those days, going to a show was a big event. Anyone improperly attired was not allowed to enter the showroom.

**myram borders:** When Elvis was here in the '50s the city was using a Western Ranch style theme and by the time he returned in the late '60s the city was growing up a little bit in the sense that it was beginning to look different. It was not as casual as it was with the Last Frontier and the El Rancho Vegas. People would go to those shows in Western clothes or casual attire. By the mid '60s women were going to shows in evening gowns and fur coats. It was starting to get ritzy and high class with diamonds and furs.

**millie kirkham:** Everybody who came to the show dressed to the nines.

**loanne miller parker:** At that beginning of Elvis's first run, the women wore cocktail dresses or formal gowns to the shows with their best jewelry and the men wore suits. It was an atmosphere of glamour that sadly no longer exists today.

**nicholas naff:** In the early months of Elvis's first appearance, his audience was mainly comprised of his fans. That's why Colonel Parker was so convinced that Elvis would sell out and he did. Then after he caught on his audience base broadened beyond his hardcore followers.

# protecting the king

Handling an artist of Elvis's caliber, elaborate security strategies were employed to protect the star from over enthusiastic fans and those with more sinister motives.

**richard moreno** (security, International Hotel, 1969-1973): The hotel security chief told us not to talk to Elvis unless he engaged us in conversation. We were told we needed to act professionally around him at all times. He arrived about a week early to do final rehearsals.

The day that our shift was required to escort him for the first time we were given a list of people that were allowed to come in Elvis's suite upstairs. It was very tight. Joe Esposito came out and said, "Guys, Elvis is getting ready to come out and we're gonna go downstairs." Soon the door opened and there was Elvis. Elvis was introduced to us and he stuck out his hand and he said, "Hi, I'm Elvis Presley." (laughs) I always thought that was funny, as if we didn't know who he was. (laughs) We got onto the service elevator—he never used the public elevators—and we went downstairs. Elvis and his friends were clowning around, punching each other the entire time. By the time we were downstairs, Elvis had included us all in the hijinks. We were scared at first because we were told to be very professional around him but after the first day that professionalism all went out the window and from then on we were part of the constant clowning around.

Sometimes fans would bribe employees and ask them to tell them his escort route and they'd plan where to hide. As we walked along the escort route, which would lead us to the main showroom dressing room, there were times we found fans hiding underneath service carts. They'd hide in bathrooms; they'd hide anywhere they could find a doorway that they could open and step inside in hopes of being able to meet Elvis. Occasionally, some lucky fans that were hiding away would see us coming down the hall and they'd pop out. Elvis would stop to meet the fans but we were instructed to keep nudging him along.

**larry muhoberac:** There was a whole cordon of police, maybe 20 or 30 hidden out of sight in the showroom. Nobody knew what was gonna happen. They were there to protect Elvis.

**sonny west:** In some way, security at a show is all a big bluff. You can put 20 or 50 police officers in front of a stage but you've got 2000 people, if more than 50 decide to rush that stage at one time, some of them are gonna get up there.

**terry blackwood:** The Memphis Mafia were the major players in his security. But there were also tons of security guards placed around the room at various locations looking out for troublemakers. He had a lot of threats on his life. I remember once a guy sent him a note saying, "I'm gonna kill you tonight. I'm gonna shoot you in the back." He was so angry that his girlfriend thought Elvis was just the greatest thing she'd ever seen. On that particular night security was extremely tight. Elvis said, "Man, I don't know who this guy is but I'm really

L-R: Lamar Fike, Charlie Hodge, Elvis, security guard Richard Moreno

scared." When he sang "You've Lost That Lovin' Feeling," he'd turn around, and the spotlight hits him right on his back. The lights are out in the auditorium and all you'd see was the back of his jumpsuit. You can imagine how nervous he was because that made him such an easy target. But fortunately this guy was just mouthing off. He did evoke a lot of envy and jealousy from men who brought their wives or girlfriends and saw the way they responded to Elvis and they didn't like it.

MILLIE KIRKHAM: A couple of times Elvis actually went out and walked through the audience in the showroom. I think his bodyguards were a little bit upset about that.

# dRESS REHEARSaL

Borrowing airfare from his mother, 18 year-old fan, Ian Fraser-Thomson arrived in Las Vegas on the day of Elvis's opening show. Dropping off his belongings at a six dollar a night fleabag hotel, he headed across the street to the International Hotel where by a twist of fate he wound up being a first-hand witness to a final dress rehearsal. Lady luck would strike a second time as the enterprising young adult was able sneak into the opening night invitation only show.

**iAN FRASER-THOMSON** (concert attendee): Although I knew that Elvis was going to be doing his opening show on August 1st, I got to Vegas a day early. Sometime in the morning I went across the street to the International and looked at all the Elvis decorations. I ended up on the second floor where there was a swimming pool, which was advertised as the second largest body of water next to Lake Mead. So I was hanging out by the pool and then I went into the restroom. When I was in there I heard Elvis music being piped in and thought, "How great!" I heard "Love Me Tender" and suddenly realized it was a version that I'd never heard before. I went, "Oh my God, it's live, Elvis must be rehearsing!" So I immediately left the restroom, went downstairs and found the showroom. There was a security guard at the front door. I watched and waited and eventually someone came up to the security guard. While he was being distracted I sneaked up a winding staircase which got me up to the balcony without being noticed. I could hear Elvis rehearsing so I crept down very low and peeked my head over the barrier. There was Elvis, dressed in black pants and puffed sleeve green shirt, sitting on a bar stool and he was just finishing "Mystery Train." I was obviously amazed. He was working through the numbers with the band and a full orchestra. He called out a few names of songs like "Memories," "Yesterday" and a couple of rock numbers. He remained seated most of the time on the bar stool in an effort to conserve his energy. Sometimes they'd run through an entire song, other times they'd work on an intro or work on the ending of a song. There was a lot of fine tuning going on. "Suspicious Minds" really sticks out in my memory because the song wasn't released yet and I'd never heard it. It was really exciting and it gave me chills. I thought, "This is a killer song."

Before they did "Suspicious Minds," Joe Esposito, Elvis's right hand man said, "Hey, there's someone up there!", pointing up at the balcony. My cover was blown. He said, "Let's get 'em!" I immediately got up and ran into the fire escape corridor and luckily found an unlocked door. It turned out to be the door entry for the person who was running the spotlight. There was a seat behind the spotlight with a clear view of the stage. That's where I hid and watched and listened to the rest of the dress rehearsal. I remember hearing Joe Esposito and another guy saying, "I think he went down here!" and they ran past the corridor and down the stairs. I breathed a big sigh of relief because I was in the clear.

I was also able to sneak into the show. After he finished the rehearsal, Elvis and the TCB band went down into the dressing room area. I was really anxious to meet Elvis and thought it might be my only chance so I left the spotlight closet, went downstairs and walked to the back of the stage where the orchestra was filing out and just blended in. I made some small talk with one of the orchestra members and tried to pretend that I belonged. I walked right past Elvis's dressing room with the big star on the door but it was already closed so I just kept walking. I followed the musicians and went into the room where the orchestra was packing up and talked more to one of the guys. He asked me, "What are you doing here?" I thought real quick and said, "I'm the understudy to Elvis's piano player." He laughed and I'm not sure how convincing I was being an 18 year-old. He asked, "Are you gonna be here tonight?" And I thought, "Tonight?" Then it struck me that Elvis was gonna be performing a show tonight before his official opening on August 1st. Anyhow, I said, "Yeah, sure, I'm gonna be here. So I'll see you later." Then what was racing through my mind was, "How am I gonna see the show?" I thought I might be able to crawl up into the catwalk where all the lights were hanging over the stage and wait up there but I nixed that idea. My second thought was maybe I should just stay and hide in that closet until the show starts but I decided that was kind of crazy. Ultimately, I decided to go back to the Riviera Apartments where I was staying. I walked around backstage by the kitchen and exited at the loading dock. I went back to the hotel, changed into a sport coat and tie and went back to the International and came in through the same way and no one stopped me. I kind of acted like I belonged. I went up those stairs and hid in that spotlight closet.

The showroom started filling up. Every now and then I left the closet and looked to see if there were any empty seats. Throughout that evening while people were eating and drinking—there was complimentary alcohol on the table—I noticed one seat close to center stage that was open. I said to myself. "Ian, this is do or die, why don't you go for it?" So I left the safety of the spotlight closet, went down the corridor and down those same stairs and went into that side entry door. As I walked in there was a security guard at the door. He said, "Can I help you?" I said, No thanks, "I've already been seated" and I walked right past with no problem. I went to center stage and plopped myself down in that seat. The table was cleared and everyone had cocktail glasses on the table. Mine was just a water glass that hadn't been touched. I took that water glass, downed the water, pulled a bottle of whiskey that was on the table and started to pour myself a drink so I could blend in. The women across from me gave me a look like, "Who the hell are you?" I said, "Oh maam, can I pour you a drink?" And she said, "Oh, thank you." Then someone said, "Well, who are you?" And I said, "I'm the understudy for Elvis's piano player." And they said, "Oh, that's cool." One person said, "If you've got something to do with Elvis, why don't you give me an autograph" and they passed me their menu. So I signed it and wrote my name so it was totally illegible. (laughs) Then someone else at the table had me sign their menu. I thought, "My God, I'm making a scene here!" and I was praying every moment for the lights to go down and finally they did. All through the time until Elvis came out on stage I was in mortal fear that someone was gonna come up and say, "What are you doing in this seat, this person's supposed to be sitting here." But that never happened and I was able to see the show and watch Elvis from ten feet away.

# STARS, STARS, STARS

A high watt coterie of celebrities assembled for the show.

**joe esposito:** For every show we had three booths reserved for celebrities or family members.

**terry blackwood:** It was the event of the century. Every star imaginable was on hand to witness Elvis's opening show.

**gloria greer** (ABC-TV local reporter): The Colonel had a home in Palm Springs and that's where I lived and where my TV show originated from. He came up to me and said, "How would you like to go to Elvis's opening night show in Las Vegas? We'll fly you up, we'll provide the TV crew and put you up in the hotel. We'd like you to interview the various celebrities that come to the opening and you can use it on your television program." Of course I said sure. (laughs) That's how it happened. So fast forward to opening night…Everyone was waiting outside the showroom and there was a lot of excitement in the air. It was a different time and era. I was the only TV reporter there doing interviews before and after the show. That night Henry Mancini told me, "This is an event. This is an event that I've looked forward to and two of my three children are here. But they wanted to come up the minute they knew he was opening. If you realize the age group Mr. Presley encompasses he is an institution but a good one. When you think about it Presley has longevity now. They said, "What does a rock and roll artist do when he's thirty?" Well, we're gonna see what he does when he's thirty because I imagine Elvis is around that age now." That night I also interviewed Ed Ames who was also appearing on the Strip so he went between his shows at The Riviera to see Elvis. I interviewed George Hamilton, Shirley Bassey, Alex Shoofey, the president of the hotel and Bill Miller, the talent booker. My piece on Elvis's opening aired the next night on my own segment on the local news called "Stars on the Desert." A short piece of it was used in the film *This is Elvis*, which shows me interviewing George Hamilton. What a kick.

**rodney bingenheimer** (music writer, *GO* magazine): I remember seeing celebrities everywhere looked. I took notes and wrote down all the people I saw: Fats Domino, Governor Pat Brown, Phil Ochs, Barbara Stanwyck, Sonny and Cher, Paul Anka, Donald O'Connor, Henry Mancini, Dionne Warwick, Johnny Rivers with Lou Adler, Mac Davis, and Herb Albert.

**terry blackwood** (The Imperials): Sammy Davis Jr. was right there in the front row center. Tom Jones. Juliet Prowse. She'd worked with him on *G.I. Blues*. They were all blown away.

**sonny west:** Cary Grant came back to see Elvis's show several times. He really liked Elvis. He'd sit in his booth and totally enjoy the show.

**joe esposito:** Elvis was an usher in the movies so he idolized those movie people that would come to the shows like Cary Grant.

# backstage jitters

Backstage, Elvis was preparing for his first show. By all accounts, he was 175 lbs of pure nerves and pumping adrenaline.

**loanne miller parker:** Elvis and the Colonel were both nervous wrecks before the show. This was a big gamble.

**alex shoofey:** Could he be successful? Nobody knew. The only one who thought he would was his manager. (UNLV Oral History Research Center, March 2003)

**t.g. sheppard:** RCA felt Elvis's show would go over big but no one really knew what to expect.

**loanne miller parker:** They couldn't be sure how the audience would respond Elvis. They were turning their backs on the movie business and they were taking a big chance, a big risk. Elvis needed it. He needed the stimulation of something different and the Colonel welcomed it because he needed it too. This was something they both wanted but there were no guarantees.

**john wilkinson:** Back in '56 they practically ran him out of town on a rail.

**d.j. fontana:** We were booked to play the Venus Room at the New Frontier Hotel with Freddie Martin and his orchestra and we had a great comedian Shecky Greene working with us.

**shecky greene** (comedian): There was a 75 foot cut out of Elvis out in front of the hotel. The hotel was fairly new and the Venus Room was a big room.

**d.j. fontana:** Freddie Martin had a great big band. They were doing the play "Oklahoma" on stage and that's what we were up against. They had this big musical with all kinds of dancing and stuff going on and we got out there with three little pieces and there wasn't enough noise (laughs).

**shecky greene:** I think they wanted Elvis to headline at the beginning but his first show was kind of disastrous. He wasn't ready for a nightclub.

**d.j. fontana:** That older crowd was used to big productions so we didn't do well.

**shecky greene:** It wasn't his crowd, it was a nightclub crowd. Elvis wasn't known to anybody in the older generation. These gamblers didn't know who the hell he was! I was a nightclub act so I went over great 'cause I talked about gambling, and everything they knew about.

**marty lacker:** You gotta remember that Vegas in '56 were nothing but old people. Parker put him in a venue and in front of an older crowd that didn't like him. They called Elvis's music "devil music."

Elvis in front of New Frontier Hotel, 1956

**shecky greene:** Bing Crosby came in to see the show and I sat with him and we watched Elvis's act. Frankly, I wasn't impressed by Elvis's show but Bing was. He said, "Mark my words, this kid will be the biggest thing in show business."

**d.j. fontana:** We did a special show on a Friday or Saturday afternoon for the kids. They let the kids into the casino, which they never do. It was just full of kids and Elvis went over well. See, that was his crowd.

**shecky greene:** They were the ones buying his records. The older crowd didn't know numbers like "Heartbreak Hotel" or "Blue Suede Shoes."

**d.j. fontana:** Elvis was disappointed we didn't go over that well in Vegas. He was still fairly new in the business so he didn't know how they operated and we surely didn't. We just didn't belong there.

**marty lacker:** From then on, he had a bad taste in his mouth about Las Vegas from his shows at the New Frontier in '56.

**t.g. sheppard:** Returning to Vegas years later, Elvis needed to prove he had staying power.

**sandi miller:** In the late '60s my roommate, Jan and I would be invited down to Elvis's Palm Springs house on the weekends. Before he signed the contract to play the International, he kept making jokes about what a flop he was when he last played in Vegas in the '50s. Because he brought it up two or three times I could sense he was worried it could happen again.

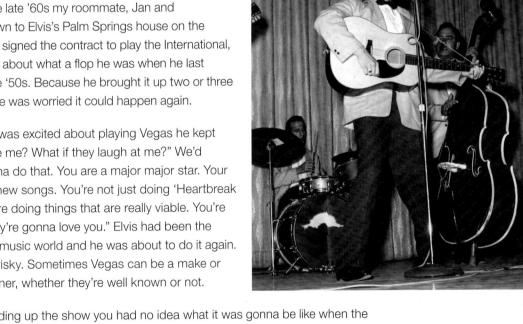

Elvis live,
New Frontier Hotel,
1956

**john wilkinson:** While he was excited about playing Vegas he kept saying, "What if they don't like me? What if they laugh at me?" We'd all say, "Elvis, they're not gonna do that. You are a major major star. Your voice is beautiful, you've got new songs. You're not just doing 'Heartbreak Hotel' and 'Hound Dog'. You're doing things that are really viable. You're gonna be fine, you watch, they're gonna love you." Elvis had been the biggest thing that ever hit the music world and he was about to do it again. But to start off in Vegas was risky. Sometimes Vegas can be a make or break situation for an entertainer, whether they're well known or not.

**joe moscheo:** Leading up the show you had no idea what it was gonna be like when the curtain goes up for the first show. You can only anticipate. We were well-rehearsed and we knew the music was gonna be good. You can see how nervous he was before a show in *That's The Way It Is*. That's the same way he was before his first Vegas show. He thought he was gonna forget the lyrics. Elvis was a pretty nervous cat anyway. He had a lot of nervous energy anyway, flipping his rings around his fingers.

**SONNY WEST:** My future wife, Judy and I flew out to see Elvis's opening show. We were seated in one of Elvis's booths and all of a sudden someone came out and said, "Elvis wants you to come backstage for a minute." So I went back there and he asked me, "Sonny, I wonder if you'll stay back here with me and stand on the side of the stage when I perform?" I stood and watched the show from the side of the stage. Before he went on Elvis said, "Watch anyone that may jump up and run up to me, I still think about that Jacksonville show." (laughs) This was back in the '50s when he played this outdoor show and tons of girls stormed the stage and ripped his clothes off.

**jerry scheff:** We had been rehearsing for weeks and we all felt excited and confident in the music. We all went down to Elvis's dressing room to hang out before the show. (Elvis Collectors Brasil)

**cissy houston:** Elvis, his band, the Sweet Inspirations and the Imperials all got into a circle and prayed together before the show. We'd do that for every show. It became one big family.

**SONNY WEST:** In the dressing room, Elvis was nervous and pacing back and forth like a panther. Wiggling his fingers, beating his fingers on the table, his foot was constantly moving and wiggling and it wouldn't stop.

**joe esposito:** He made all of us nervous just by being around him. We didn't know what to say to him the last hour before the opening show.

**chris hutchins:** He was really in a state. At one stage he was saying he couldn't go through with it and Joe Esposito calmed him down and told him and said, "It's gonna be great, it's gonna be fantastic."

**elvis presley:** I've never gotten over what they call stage fright. I go through it every show. Before I go on stage I'm pretty much thinking about the show. I never get completely comfortable with it at any given time and I don't let the people with me get too comfortable with it. I remind them that it's a new crowd out there, they haven't seen us before so it's gotta be like the first time. (*Elvis on Tour* interview)

**joe moscheo:** He'd read the telegrams people sent him, "Break a leg" or "Have a great show." The guys were all around trying to keep him calm. Some of the time he'd walk across the hall to our dressing room and ask how we were doing. He'd try to make us feel good. If he wanted to break into a gospel song we'd move over into the bathroom in the dressing room where it was all tile. We'd sing something just to hear the resonance of that sound in the bathroom and that would relax him. He was wound up for that first show and was wandering around like a caged tiger.

**bobby morris:** Before the show I went backstage and my dressing room was next to the comedian Sammy Shore. Elvis came into my dressing room and we were walking towards the stage. He asked me who was in the audience. I told him who was there and he said, "Bobby, I'm a little uptight about it, all those big stars?" I said, "Don't be nervous, just make believe that everybody sitting in the audience has no clothes on." (laughs)

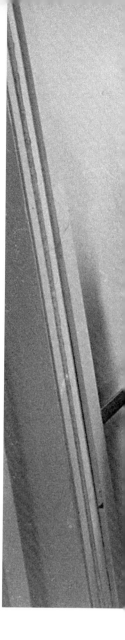

**james burton:** It was his first live show in eight years and it was a big challenge coming back. He'd be doing movies for so long and was very insecure about how his fans would accept him. Elvis came up to me right before the show and said, "James, I'm so nervous, I don't know if I can do this." I said, "Elvis, when you walk out there and the curtain goes up, after the first two or three songs it'll be like sitting at home in your living room."

**lamar fike:** I always called Elvis a gunslinger. He might have been nervous, but once he put his guns on he did what he did best.

**john wilkinson:** When the curtain was ready to go up, he was visibly shaking but he was ready. You could see the nervous anxiety in his eyes. I told him, "If you get lost, just turn around and we'll start playing louder. Don't worry about it, your friends are here."

**john wilkinson:** Elvis looked at the Celtic cross that I had on, he clutched it in his hand and said, 'I'm glad you're here John.' (*Memories: On the Road with Elvis and John Wilkinson*/Peter Verbruggen)

# OPENING NIGHT: july 31, 1969

Dressed in a jet black jumpsuit designed by Bill Belew, Elvis opened with a spirited take of Carl Perkins' "Blue Suede Shoes." Elvis's magnificent performance was hailed by the likes of *Rolling Stone, Newsweek, Billboard* and the *New York Times* as an unequivocal triumph. Borrowing the title from his acclaimed first 1960 post-Army album, on that historic night, Elvis was most certainly back.

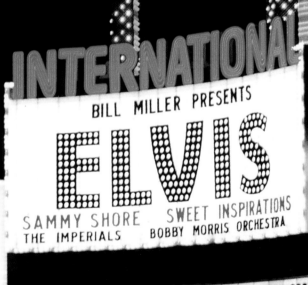

**bruce banke:** Elvis's opening performance on July 31 was by invitation only with most of the prime seats held for casino VIP players and the press.

**bobby morris:** For the first show everybody was comped. They were all guests of Kirk Kerkorian.

**rodney bingenheimer:** I was writing for a free national music newspaper called *GO* magazine. Nick Naff, the publicity director for the International Hotel, arranged for me to cover Elvis's opening show. He provided two tickets and I brought Screaming Lord Sutch, a British rock and roll singer. We sat at the third table from the front. Rock columnist May Mann was at our table. She later did a book on Elvis. On all the tables was a gift box set—and I still have it. Inside were two record albums— *Elvis in Memphis* and *Elvis*, the soundtrack for the '68 TV special, a bio, a color photo of Elvis, a program and a '69 calendar

**hank delespinasse** (*Newsweek* photographer): I was working for *Newsweek* on assignment to shoot Elvis's opening. Photographers from around the world were on hand to capture the event and access was very restricted. Everyone showed up thinking we'd be able to photograph Elvis close to the stage but they made all the photographers shoot from the balcony. Shooting him from a distance presented a challenge. Unlike most of the other photographers who came from out of town, I lived in Vegas so I was able to go home and bring a few longer telephoto lenses which enabled me to capture the action.

**myrna smith:** We opened the show and did a short set.

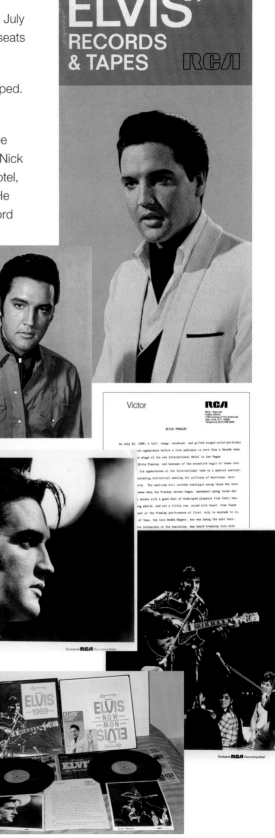

**ESTELLE BROWN:** We were somewhat apprehensive whether we'd be accepted or not. That was a little scary. We'd do a few songs, three at the most. Sometimes we'd sing "The Impossible Dream" and we'd do "Sweet Inspiration" too.

**MYRNA SMITH:** The audience was very good to us. We knew that they were there for Elvis and we knew they wanted us to get off the stage as fast as possible so they could see him. So we made sure we kept the show short. We didn't want to get booed off the stage. (laughs)

**TERRY BLACKWOOD:** Then the comedian, Sammy Shore came on. People gave him polite applause but that's it.

**LOANNE MILLER PARKER:** Colonel wanted a family show so Sammy was given instructions that his comedy could not have nasty language and would have to be suitable for children. Sammy did the best he could, but it was a tough audience. (laughs)

**BRUCE BANKE:** Sammy Shore had one of the most difficult assignments ever, not unlike presenting pencil drawings prior to a Rembrandt exhibit. The capacity crowd wanted to see the King and wasn't ashamed to let everyone know it.

**SAMMY SHORE:** I always came out with some kind of crazy opening. I wouldn't come out and say "Good evening, I'm Sammy Shore, it's really nice to be here at the International Hotel." Instead of doing that I'd come out dribbling a basketball and say "What time are the Knicks showing up?" Or I'd come out as a Russian ballet dancer. The crowd would think, "What is this?" It caught their attention. The first night I opened for Elvis I just walked out there and grabbed the mike and it was dead. No sound.

2500 people there did not want to see me or anybody else for that matter. They didn't care about the Sweet Inspirations, they didn't know who I was. They couldn't have cared less. It was a tough crowd. When I walked out there it was a dud. If I had four people applaud me that was a lot. So I started my set and I panicked because the mike was dead. What are you gonna do? I'm out here in front of all the wolves and they're gonna throw me to the lions if I don't get out of this one. I started kibbitzing around with the mike cord. A few minutes later the backstage crew put another microphone out there and I knew that one worked. But I pretended that it didn't work and pantomimed it. Finally I said, "They spent 53 million dollars on a hotel and fourteen dollars on a microphone." I started ad-libbing, reciting Shakespeare and I finally got 'em. If that didn't happen to me I would have probably gone right into the crapper.

It was always tough to win over his audience. They came to see Elvis and were so excited to be there that my job was difficult. Nobody really knew who I was. It was a tough position for anyone who opened for him. Anyone would have had a tough time, I don't care who it was. I viewed it as a challenge to win them over. I never let things like that get me down. I'm a fighter and have always been that way. If I can't get 'em with the left I'll get 'em with the right.

So I walked off the stage after my act and Elvis was standing there white as a ghost. He was scared to death. I shook his hand and his hand was wet as ice. I told him that the audience was waiting for him and that he was gonna do great. But you could see it in his face that he was petrified.

August 1, 1969

Opening night, July 31, 1969

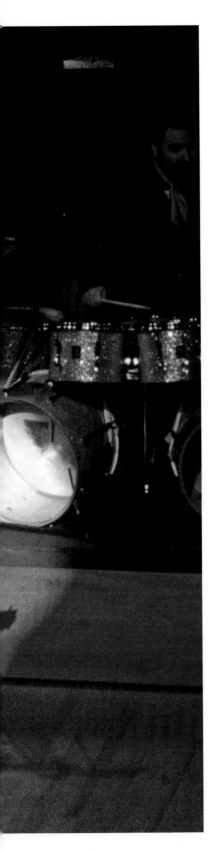

**loanne miller parker:** Even before Elvis came out on stage there was an energy that I have never felt anywhere else.

**terry blackwood:** The crowd knew it was time for Elvis and this was what they'd all been waiting for. They were on the edge of their seats and ready to see the man they'd wanted to see all of their lives.

**ian fraser-thomson:** When the lights were dimmed the crowd was unsettled, almost agitated and loud and then when the horns and the band ignited in the famous intro, the crowd was temporarily silenced.

**joe moscheo:** We got the call and went up onstage to get into our places on stage left. He walked out on our side and gave us a wink.

**bruce banke:** As the house lights went down and the 10,000-pound gold lamé, Austrian-made draped curtain slowly rose, Elvis walked out on stage completely unannounced. Stars were usually introduced by an off-stage announcer but the Colonel had other ideas. He told me, "When the audience comes to see a show, they know who they are there to see. If someone has to tell them who you are, you are definitely not a star."

**loanne miller parker:** Colonel told me that he and Elvis had a conversation about that. In Vegas, they'd have a drum roll or crashing chord and then the announcer would say, "Ladies and gentlemen, here's…"

**joe moscheo:** He walked out and it was pandemonium, all the flashbulbs and the cheers, the screaming.

**james burton:** The audience was so incredibly loud—stompin', screaming and beatin' on the tables. The crowd was goin' nuts.

**john wilkinson:** They wouldn't shut up, all through the first song they kept shouting and cheering, they couldn't get enough of him. It was amazing, that thunderous applause coming from one showroom. Elvis turned around, laughed and shook his shoulders, as if he was saying: 'this isn't so bad after all.' (*Memories: On the Road with Elvis and John Wilkinson*/Peter Verbruggen)

**bruce banke:** Elvis grabbed the microphone, hit a typical Elvis spread-legged stance from the '50s, and his knees started to twitch. Before he could sing a note, the audience exploded, giving him a rousing standing ovation, even climbing on chairs and screaming so loud the chandeliers rattled.

**ian fraser-thomson:** He reached out with his right hand to take the microphone to sing the first words of the evening and his hand was noticeably shaking back and forth. Holy smokes, Elvis was trembling! He was scared to death. Then came "Well, its one for the money, two for the show…" and off Elvis went.

**bobby morris:** During the song he turned around and gave me a look like "Yeah, this is gonna be fun."

**bruce banke:** He was nervous at first but quickly hit his groove and gave a performance that had the critics raving. It was also the Colonel who advised Elvis not to do any encores. "Always leave them wanting more."

**bill jost** (assistant maître d', International Hotel showroom): I watched the audience as he walked out on stage, and so many had their faces in their hands. They'd sit there and cry. It was almost Biblical, as if the clouds had parted and down a shaft of light came the angels.

**priscilla presley:** When he walked out on that stage it was magical. The energy was incredible. He was like this tiger on stage that was unchained. It was like watching an animal unfold in front of your eyes with this magnetism that drew everyone in. I'm sitting there in the first row seeing him perform and my mouth dropped open, "My God, it's a totally different Elvis." You saw him on the '68 special but now he even unfolded more and started to be who he is and where Elvis felt the most comfortable was on stage. What was really amazing for me is I'd never really seen his performing side. I only saw what he did in movies, which you can't really say is performing. It's staged. It's choreographed. It's not really him being who he is. It's not him being the emotional, passionate singer. It's more of this is what he needed to do, this was a job. But when you saw him onstage that first night you saw who he was as an entertainer. And there's nothing or never will be anything like it.

**elvis presley** (dialogue with crowd): I'd like to thank you for coming out. This is my first live appearance in nine years. Appeared dead a few times, but I really like it and I hope you do too.

**cricket mendell coulter** (fan): Opening night was not filled with fans, but mainly press, VIPs and celebrities and they're not easy to impress. There were some people there who thought he was gonna bomb because he'd been away so long. But almost immediately, he had everyone right in the palm of his hand.

**david stanley:** I was a 13-year old kid into the Beatles, the Stones and Led Zeppelin. I was listening to everything but him. I didn't look at Elvis as a rock and roll star. All of a sudden Elvis comes out and throws down and that was it. After living at Graceland since 1960 and growing up with Elvis, that night I became a fan.

**dave clark** (The Dave Clark Five): When I saw Elvis for the first time in Vegas I went in expecting the impossible because he changed all of our lives. In England and in Europe he was the one responsible for turning us onto rock and roll. He was as good as I expected him to be and even better. He was magic. To me, Elvis was the ultimate performer in rock and roll.

**glen campbell:** There wasn't anybody like Elvis. I've never seen anybody with that much charisma. He turned the whole town upside down. His show was fabulous. Elvis might have been limited on the guitar playing three chords but boy could he sing! He was just a phenomenal talent. At the show there were 50 year-old and 60 year-old women screaming like teenagers, (shouts loudly) "I LOVE YOU ELVIS!" He showed that he still had it.

**MAC DAVIS** (songwriter, "In The Ghetto"): All the guys including me couldn't believe what was happening. The women in that room went totally insane. All of them—married, young, old—they went crazy. The ones that didn't jump up and run to the end of the stage were sitting there going, "I wish I wasn't with my husband now 'cause I'd run to the stage." (laughs) I had a grin from ear to ear because I'd never seen anything like this.

> **STEVE BINDER:** When I saw him in Vegas it was an extension where he was building on what we had done on the '68 special.

**DAVID STANLEY:** Elvis personified cool that night. He was just lethal.

> **RONNIE TUTT:** The energy was incredible. He was like a cat let out of a cage. (Elvis Australia/www.elvis.com.au/Arjan Deelen)

August 1, 1969

Opening night, July 31, 1969

**jerry scheff:** When we finished the first song he knew the people still loved him. (Elvis Collectors Brasil)

**james burton:** It gave you chills to see the excitement onstage and watch how much the audience was lovin' the show. We played like there was no tomorrow. All the musicians were glowing. It was just the most incredible feeling. Elvis has so much security with the band that he felt he could go out there and do anything and that was a good feeling for him.

**rona barrett:** Among the press, Elvis had a reputation of being someone you should never count out. It was a make or break evening for Elvis. There was a big curiosity factor among the crowd.

**chris hutchins:** Elvis had something to prove that night but I don't think even he was certain it would go so well. Parker wasn't sure that he could pull it off and Elvis surprised him. It was the same thing that happened on that television show that Elvis did with the black leather. Parker fought him bitterly on that and lost.

**bill medley** (The Righteous Brothers): Elvis knew that he got off the track with all those movies and people like Tom Jones and these other sex symbols were coming along. I think Elvis needed to jump back out there and find out if he was still the guy.

**david stanley:** Of course Vernon was nervous because that was his son. There was that sense that this show could make or break Elvis. Vernon represented the whole mindset of the entire audience.

**larry muhoberac:** You could tell there was a lot on the line for the first show. You could feel that the audience was gonna explode. Once he came out on stage the whole place went berserk! It was like a wall of sound with people clapping and screaming and yelling.

**david stanley:** Vernon was elated. His son was back.

**t.g. sheppard:** It was almost as if he waved his hand through the air you could almost see an opening, like the air was cut. He had such a charisma onstage. Compared to his shows in the '50s, he was more seasoned. Back then he was real raw and electrifying. This time it was a major production with the orchestration and the backing singers.

Opening night, July 31, 1969

**elvis presley:** A live concert to me is exciting because of all the electricity that is generated in the crowd and on stage. My favorite part of the business is a live concert. (Aloha from Hawaii press conference, Las Vegas, 1972)

**kirk kerkorian:** Elvis just tore the place down. He was just a house breaker. His show was fantastic. It was one of the most exciting shows I've ever seen.

**marty lacker:** He put everything he had into his performance. He wanted to erase what had happened in '56 and show everybody that, "Hey motherfuckers, I'm back!" He was never better than on that first engagement in Vegas.

**george klein:** He was doing what he loved most of all, which was performing in front of a live audience. He had all this talent that had been held back for eight years while he was making movies and he just exploded onstage again.

**lance legault** (Elvis's friend and movie stunt double): I played tambourine on the side of the stage for the sit down jam session on the '68 Comeback show and if anything topped that special, it was his performance on opening night. It was as good as I've ever seen him. He was wired. No gingerbread, no frills, he just sang and went to work. He was home, he was where he needed to be.

**bruce banke:** The audience was jammed with celebrities as well, people like Ann-Margret, Angie Dickinson and Burt Bacharach, Dick Clark, Petula Clark, George Hamilton, Bobby Vinton, Carol Channing, Wayne Newton, Paul Anka, Shirley Bassey, Pat Boone, Cary Grant, Fats Domino, Henry Mancini and Sammy Davis Jr. who led a standing ovation.

**fats domino:** I loved the show. He was a great entertainer. Nobody ever did it like he did it. I loved his voice too. It was different than anybody else. There won't be another Elvis.

**george hamilton:** I grew up with Elvis's music, songs like "Don't Be Cruel" and "Blue Suede Shoes" so here I was coming to face to face with the guy whose music I'd play while dating my girlfriend in school. That night was his comeback to Vegas and it set a precedent.

August 1, 1969

**TOM JONES:** It was tremendous to see him. That was Elvis at his peak as far as I was concerned. He was as hot then as he ever was before. His voice was still as strong, he looked great, he performed great and he was Elvis Presley once again. He was fantastic, he couldn't have been better. Watching him perform in '69, I noticed certain moves that he did, which might have been inspired by what I was doing at the time, which was a huge compliment, and also some of his phrasing on the records changed slightly. I could hear things that I had sort of done. (laughs) But he admitted to it and said "You've influenced me and inspired me." And I said, "Well, that's fantastic" because in the '50s I was listening to Elvis Presley records and that's what started me off. He's the main reason why I started singing. So it was great that I could contribute something to him after what he had given to me.

**JOHNNY RIVERS:** I first saw Elvis, Scotty and Bill in '55 at Baton Rouge high school. He was so different from everybody else. You knew he was gonna be a star. So when I saw him again for that opening show in '69 he was a little bit more subdued. He wasn't a hopped up teenager anymore but he showed up to rock. Elvis was always dynamic onstage There was an electric energy about him. He proved he was the biggest star in the world.

**BOBBY VINTON:** Elvis was like an institution. He just walked on the stage and the people stood and the girls were crying. I've seen Frank Sinatra, the Beatles and Michael Jackson and I've never seen anything like the reaction Elvis had on an audience.

**GEORGE HAMILTON:** He had that power to command a stage. He looked incredible. and he was in the best shape of his entire life.

**PETULA CLARK:** He was extremely handsome so as soon as he walked on the stage you were blown away by this beautiful man. They have an expression in French. Elvis was a *bête de la scène*. That's somebody who was a stage animal and you could tell that night that's what Elvis was born to do. There was a great animal magnetism in the way he sang, the way he moved, and the way he smiled. And he was funny. A man who is that handsome and that sexy with a sense of humor is irresistible. (laughs) He was the epitome of what a true star should be.

**CAROL CHANNING:** Elvis was spectacular. I loved it and was carried away by his wonderful performance.

**PAT BOONE:** I brought my daughter, Debby to see him. He came out onstage and rocked everybody. His performance announced in no uncertain terms that he was back and he was "Mr. Big". Debby was blown away by it. She remembered the guy who used to come over to the house. He was just a good looking friend of Daddy's. It was truly a sensory blitz—the volume, the rhythmic excitement, his dynamism, and command of the stage. That first night was very very exciting. He's always been an exciting performer and for that show he stepped it up considerably. He wore the Bill Belew clothes and he kept punching the air with karate moves. He didn't do that in the '50s, but he did it now. His show, by comparison to what I did onstage, was so over the top. I greatly admired it. I was appearing at the Sahara Hotel and he was appearing at the International. I drew big crowds too but I didn't try to do that all out, high decibel, spectacle kind of a show. I wore a tuxedo and did some rock and roll, and sang some ballads and other pop songs of the day. I was "Mr. Straight;" I was salt and he was pepper. But it worked out for both of us.

**JOE MOSCHEO:** From a musical standpoint, in particular, we were so impressed with his voice. We were blown away by how good he was.

**MYRNA SMITH:** The emotion that he put into his songs was so powerful.

**ESTELLE BROWN:** A lot of people sing today and they're just singing words and they're not really into what they're singing. He meant every word he sang and you could feel it.

**JOE MOSCHEO:** Elvis surprised us with his range and his stamina. He'd worked so hard and put one hundred percent into those early performances to the point that you didn't believe. Where did that come from? How did he do it?

**SONNY WEST:** There was so much electricity bouncing off of him that I felt electrified, like a lighting bolt. My feet were off the floor, it was like I was levitating. (laughs)

**john wilkinson:** You can't even put the energy and excitement level of opening night on a scale. It was off the charts. It was so exciting watching this living legend go out onstage and do it again. I think he knew he had it in him. He just needed to prove it to himself and to his audience.

**joe esposito:** After the first two songs, there was no holding him back. The love he got from the audience pushed him even more.

**petula clark:** I'd heard through the grapevine that Elvis was nervous for the show so I felt a little bit apprehensive for him because I wanted him to be wonderful. You didn't want anything to go wrong for him. But his performance was much much better than I expected and he sang much better than I thought he would. With somebody like Elvis, you also sensed it was much more than just going to see a performance. It was a true happening. It was also about being in the presence of this legend.

**sammy shore:** It was like Jesus coming down the mountain.

**bobby vinton:** It was a dynamic thing to see him. I think all the women in the place were in love with him and so were the men. People of all ages loved Elvis, which is rare. You had the teenagers and then you had the grandmothers too. Elvis had everything. He had the looks, he had the voice, and he had the soul.

**terry blackwood:** I've never been in a situation since where it was that exciting. He appeared to be in control but you hadn't seen him backstage before he went on, he was just nervous as a cat. His hands were trembling and he was pacing.

**marty lacker:** He was like a panther, he was like a big cat that pranced from side to side on the stage while he was singing and while he was talking.

**dave clark:** I liked Elvis in the very early days because he was very raw. When I saw him that night there was still a raw energy and an air of danger about him.

**joe moscheo:** He had a real intensity the first few times he played Vegas. He was really motivated and wanted to prove something to himself. He loved that the shows were so successful and that his fans still loved him. He was starved for this kind of attention because of the long movie commitment he had. Just to be in front of his fans again, to hear them, see 'em, and touch 'em, he just loved it.

**joe moscheo:** It was hard to get him off the stage. The casino wanted a 75-minute show, sometimes he'd do an hour an a half.

**lamar fike:** I did the lighting for Elvis's show. Hugo Granada taught me a lot about lights. He was probably the best light man that hit Vegas. One thing I learned was it was best for Elvis to wear a white outfit 'cause white is easier to light. For the opening show he wore black. But he didn't like it because he didn't like mohair because it ripped too easily, so he quit using it.

**rona barrett:** The show was so exciting that I almost turned into one of those screaming fans too. (laughs)

Opening night, July 31, 1969

**bobby morris:** There must have been two or three hundred girls a night that would tip Emilio, the maître d', a hundred dollars each so they could sit up front and be kissed by him. Women would rush the stage and hope for a kiss or to get one of his scarves. It was wild. I've worked with a lot of big stars but I've never seen this kind of reaction. And it would happen night after night.

**patti parry** (Elvis's personal friend): The girls would grab his hands and take off his rings. So they ended up putting band-aids around his fingers so they couldn't get the rings off.

**emilio muscelli:** There was more of a show off the stage than on the stage. The ladies would throw their room keys on the stage, panties, everything. (laughs)

**nicholas naff:** (Tom) Jones was among the horniest men I ever knew. Elvis couldn't project that sex image. But he could say to females, "Love me, I'm the nicest guy in the world." That's the very reason they love him today. He played on his own projected qualities, the nice guy, the shy guy. (*Cult Vegas*, Mike Weatherford)

**bruce banke:** During the show Colonel stood backstage, grinning from ear to ear.

**chris hutchins:** Parker was watching the show in the wings and knew then that for once the artist had taken control of his career and made the right decision.

**lamar fike:** The audience never sat down, they stood up the whole show. It was one standing ovation after the other.

**bobby morris:** The crowd just ate up every word, every note that he sang. Elvis was a natural showman. As a vocalist, his style and feel were unique. He was an originator. When he was singing you knew it was Elvis.

**rona barrett:** Elvis was one of those few performers who had *it*. His ability to communicate and connect with his audience was unparalleled.

**george klein:** Performing in a 2,000 seat showroom enabled him to have tremendous contact with his audience whereas back in the '50s he played five and ten thousand seat venues and didn't have that intimacy.

**steve binder:** Whenever you're doing live performance, half of the performance is dependent upon the audience and the other half is your performance onstage. The audience was as electrifying to Elvis as he was back to them. It was one of those magical moments that you pray for.

**elvis presley:** If I do something good they let me know and if I don't they let me know that… it's a give and take proposition in that they give me back the inspiration. I work absolutely to them, whether it's six or six thousand people, it doesn't really matter. They bring it out of me— the inspiration, the ham. (laughs) (*Elvis on Tour*, interview)

**patti parry:** It was a different Elvis at home. But when he was onstage he was *Elvis Presley*. He loved being onstage, that's what made him the happiest.

**john wilkinson:** Elvis had such a versatile voice. He could have sung opera. Nobody can touch him.

**glen d. hardin** (piano, TCB band): He was the one of the best singers there ever was. He was very gifted. But he always had a humble nature about him. I'm not sure he ever really knew how good he was. He didn't quite understand why the whole world was crazy about him.

**jackie deshannon:** Elvis's humility and his love for his fans really impressed me. That was who he was. I'm always impressed with someone who wears their crown well and he truly did.

**john wilkinson:** Everything was honest and sincere and right out front. He could take a song like "Hound Dog" and you'd believe that he was a kid in the hills singing it around the campfire. You just simply believed everything he sang.

**armond morales:** You felt the soul of the man when he sang and that's what people liked.

**millie kirkham:** When he sang to a huge audience everybody in that audience felt he was singing directly to them. He had that gift of being able to reach the audience and that's something I don't think you learn. You either have it or you don't.

**james burton:** He had pretty close to what you call perfect pitch. When he'd do "Mystery Train" he'd start singing it and it would be in the original key that he cut the record. From the bass singing up to the tenor singing, Elvis had incredible range and soulfulness.

**jerry schilling:** I never thought that Elvis could ever do anything better than when I first saw him live in 1954, '55. That was the magic. That was the wildness. That was the unpredictability. By the time he went to Vegas for those first shows, I knew that as a singer his voice has gotten better and matured. I loved it in the beginning because it was wild and it was different. Watching him in Vegas that first weekend not only did he maintain the unpredictability and the wildness he exceeded it.

**rodney bingenheimer:** On the table was a sheet of paper, which had that night's set list. I have the set list right in front of me and here's what it says:

Blue Suede Shoes
I Got a Woman
One Night
Love Me Tender
Medley: Jailhouse Rock/Don't Be Cruel/
Heartbreak Hotel/All Shook Up/Hound Dog
Memories
Can't Help Falling In Love
My Babe
I Can't Stop Loving You
In The Ghetto
Suspicious Minds
Yesterday
Hey Jude
Johnny B. Goode
Mystery Train
Tiger Man
What I'd Say

I remember that all of those songs were played on the first night. Not only that but I had a cassette player and I recorded the show. I'm not sure where that cassette is, it might be lost.

**joe esposito:** He knew they were all coming to hear him sing the songs he made famous. It was a hard hitting show with energetic numbers and great ballads. He really worked his butt out there. I don't think anybody in the world sang gospel songs in a Vegas showroom but Elvis would sing a couple during his show and people loved it. The great thing about Elvis's shows is that they were all different because that's the kind of guy he was. He'd do what he felt. He'd open up with a specific song and always close with "Can't Help Falling in Love" but besides those two, he could do anything he wanted. He could change things in the middle and with his great band they'd go right along with him. Sometimes he'd launch into a song the band didn't even know and just sit at the piano and start playing.

**cissy houston:** I took it upon myself to put soprano obligato onto some of his songs. I did that with "Are You Lonesome Tonight?" because I loved that song. Obligato is an echo of a melody that doesn't have to be the melody. It's basically a high harmony that goes with it. It gives it a good feeling and Elvis really liked it. I did that on Aretha's (Franklin) song "Ain't No Way."

**nicholas naff:** We had a lot of press at the opening show because we wanted word to get out around the world about Elvis's phenomenal success.

**ANN MOSES** (editor, *Tiger Beat* magazine/Hollywood correspondent for *New Musical Express*): I was constantly being contacted by the marketing people at RCA. They wanted coverage in *Tiger Beat* but Elvis was not popular with *Tiger Beat* readers. They were more interested in Davy Jones of the Monkees or David Cassidy. But as a courtesy I'd occasionally slip in an Elvis news item in my column like for his movie, *Speedway.* I was a big Elvis fan in the '50s but by the late '60s I was more into groups like the Beatles, the Rolling Stones and Jefferson Airplane. Then one day RCA sent me two tickets to Elvis's Comeback TV special. After seeing that show, I was totally back into Elvis. He was hip again. The next year RCA gave me press passes for Elvis's opening night show in Vegas. Let me tell you, I saw the Beatles at the Hollywood Bowl and the Rolling Stones at the Cow Palace in San Francisco. But there was something about that night that was so special. The overall excitement in the room was overwhelming. It was like you were holding your breath. Being so close to the stage and hearing that voice live was sensational. Every aspect of his performance was dead-on. Everyone was dumbstruck and didn't want the night to end. It was one of the greatest shows I've ever seen.

**david dalton** (music writer, *Rolling Stone*): I went to the Monterey Pop Festival, Woodstock and Altamont. I covered the Manson story for *Rolling Stone*, all this insane stuff. So to cover Elvis's first live show in many years was a must see for me. I flew out to Vegas for Elvis's first show with some friends from New York including Tony Secunda who managed Marianne Faithful, T-Rex, Procol Harum and The Move, and Jon Goodchild, the art director for *Rolling Stone*. My wife and I took synthesized psilocybin so we were tripping when the show was happening.

Elvis was still a huge idol. We saw him as a god. It was a quasi-religious experience. This guy who started the whole thing was back again. The show itself was very vivid and very visceral. Maybe we kid ourselves that you actually have supersonic hearing when you're on psilocybin but I actually believe you do. I could hear Elvis saying things that he wasn't speaking into the microphone. We thought we were tuning into this intimate spectral vibe of his.

Elvis was absolutely amazing. It was both an experience and a musical event. The music was great and the band was really tight. The King had returned. It felt like he had been reborn. He was feeding off of all the energy of the fans who were thrilled to see him back.

It was one of those wonderful symbiotic events where the audience and the star are both creating a combined energy field. Elvis was getting off on it. It was like some sort of a strange play starring this little kid from Tupelo, Mississippi who was made King. That show was a really ecstatic event for me to witness.

This was the old Las Vegas. It was very very garish and seedy. Neon. Kind of a like kitsch version of hell but inside the International Hotel that night there was a little bit of heaven with Elvis. It wasn't like seeing the Stones or The Who or Hendrix where it was more underground. Elvis's show was a total Hollywood glitz and glamour event but in a way it was totally appropriate for Elvis. I was thrilled *Rolling Stone* chose to run my review as an Elvis cover story.

**don short:** I was traveling with the Beatles and the Rolling Stones and writing about them so that's why they commissioned me to cover Elvis's comeback. I was at the very first show and reviewed it for the London *Daily Mirror.* Hearing him sing live rather than listening to one of his records was really exciting. It was a great moment in rock and roll history. I was impressed by Elvis's energy and versatility. The man was a living legend. As soon as the show was finished I filed my copy to London. My story ran on the front cover of the newspaper and we did two pages inside. Elvis was always very very big news everywhere around the world.

**FRANK LIEBERMAN:** Elvis was magnificent on opening night but there was a controlled mass hysteria and to be honest, opening night, which was by special invitation only, wasn't as exciting as the shows that followed on that first engagement. It wasn't a case of someone being there because they were a big gambler and got free tickets to the show. The real appreciation came the longer Elvis played there because more of his true fans were finally able to get to see him.

**GLEN D. HARDIN** (piano, TCB band): Elvis gave us the freedom to play the songs any way we wanted to. He didn't tell us to play it exactly like the record. He was very good about that. He let us play everything our way. The only time he might interfere a little bit was if we weren't playing something the way he liked it. And the funny thing is he could always tell you what was missing for him. But we did kind of play those old records the way they were because it sounded great to play them that way.

**TERRY BLACKWOOD:** Elvis knew he had an obligation to sing the songs that got him there. He didn't really enjoy a lot of the '50s songs. He hated "Hound Dog" but people wanted to hear them so he would do those kind of songs to please his fans, but (laughing) he'd make them as short and as fast as he could so he could move into songs that he really enjoyed.

**BOBBY MORRIS:** He'd done those songs in the '50s. Man, this was a new era, this was a new thing so those songs didn't interest him as much.

**RONNIE TUTT:** It was a psychological thing. Those years he wasn't necessarily proud of anymore, he'd evolved into a totally different man. He'd become very self educated, very well read, and had a whole career, years in Hollywood. A lot of water had come and gone under the bridge in his life. He was a pretty raw, wild individual in those days, so he wasn't necessarily proud of what he called "those spastic days." (The Elvis Touch/July 2002)

**JAMES BURTON:** He wanted to go further with his music. He wanted to stretch out and do songs with an orchestra; he wanted to do songs by the Beatles, Frank Sinatra tunes.

**MAC DAVIS:** I went to see him when he opened in Vegas after "In the Ghetto" was a hit. It was really exciting for me. I sat fairly close to the front row. As part of the Nancy Sinatra Revue we followed him in at the hotel. He came out onstage and said, "This is my first number one record in a while" and then he looked at me and went, "Hiya, Mac." (laughs) To me it was like the President of the United States had decorated me with a medal for valor. (laughs) I was so excited that he acknowledged me because he was such a hero to me. Just the fact that he said "Hi Mac" in front of all these people was incredible.

**MARIA COLUMBUS:** He debuted "Suspicious Minds" at that opening show and we hadn't heard it before. It was incredible. It was the longest song of the night by far and he put a lot of physicality and energy into it. The audience went crazy.

**john wilkinson:** "Suspicious Minds" showed off the range of his voice and he got to do all those exciting body movements.

**felton jarvis** (Elvis's producer): He was all over that stage. I mean, he almost hurt himself. He was doing flips and cartwheels and all that kind of stuff; on "Suspicious Minds" he'd be down on one knee and do a flip across the stage and just roll.

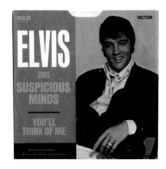

**mark james** (songwriter, "Suspicious Minds"): I was in Vegas for his first engagement and "Suspicious Minds" was headed up the charts and on its way to becoming a big hit. He invited me to the show and introduced me that night, "We've got a great song-writer in the audience…Mark James." For me, it was so wonderful to see him perform a song that I'd written. What a once in a life-time experience! You could tell right away that the song meant more to than him than just being a hit record. He put everything into it, the emotion, the passion and all the choreography with his karate moves. It became his song.

**terry blackwood:** "Suspicious Minds"' brought the house down. You have to remember the radio version and live version weren't that similar. The radio version was much slower and when he'd sing it live it was much faster. He knew when we did it live it needed more energy and he really drove the tempo.

**myrna smith:** Elvis loved singing it and over time it just got faster and faster and faster. (laughs)

**larry muhoberac:** "Suspicious Minds" was the song that got everybody in the audience going. "Mystery Train" would sometimes do that too. "In The Ghetto," also caught the attention of the audience for different reasons. They seemed to really connect with the emotion of the song.

**myrna smith:** You could tell when he loved a song because he really got into it and he would lose himself in the song. He liked singing ballads more because they showed off more of his voice and range than on the faster songs.

**terry blackwood:** The set was a good mix of up-tempo songs and ballads. He was in his thirties and there were nights I was not up for a show, and I was younger and just out of college. Here I was watching Elvis give two shows a night and it was hard for him, especially on the up-tempo tunes. I'd imagine he'd sweat off five pounds a night. For a guy in his mid-thirties to do this there was a natural inclination that he couldn't keep this pace up. I think he started to gravitate more to ballads, which allowed him to coast a little bit and let him catch his breath. After you've done "Suspicious Minds" and some of these other up-tempo songs you need a break.

**james burton:** Elvis was not limited to any style of music. He could do any style. He loved the horns and big orchestra sound. It really gave him a chance to stretch out and show the world that he could sing and do that kind of music.

**bobby morris:** Over time his shows changed, it was more of a diversified musical bag. They were less rock and roll and he did more ballads, He wanted to prove he wasn't just a rock singer but a tremendous ballad singer too. He loved doing ballads more than anything else. Elvis liked things that were dramatic. As a conductor, I wanted the introductions and the endings to the songs to be very exciting and have tremendous impact. He wanted beautiful lush sounds from the orchestra. You can hear that sound on "The Wonder of You". It's a beautiful ballad and we put a 12/8 feel to it so it had dynamics and some excitement to it.

**terry blackwood:** In early Vegas shows, Elvis would do songs made famous by other people like "Polk Salad Annie" by Tony Joe White or "Bridge Over Troubled Water" by Simon & Garfunkel. He loved those songs and made them his own. I'd say his version of "Bridge Over Troubled Water" is as popular as Simon & Garfunkel's version, at least to the Elvis crowds that we'd sing to.

**paul simon:** I saw Elvis perform "Bridge Over Troubled Water" live at Madison Square Garden and it's the only time I ever saw him. That was great fun. To watch Elvis Presley onstage singing my song was pure enjoyment.

**lamar fike:** When Elvis got nervous, he wouldn't sing, he'd talk.

**patti parry:** During those early shows he did a monologue about his career. He was a little nervous and he stuttered. But he was glad to be back and wanted to share and talk to the people about his life.

**dave clark:** I liked it when he would talk to the audience because you got to know him. He wasn't doing scripted Vegas patter in between songs. He'd open up and speak about his life. It made you get to know him more. You felt a sense of the human being behind the star, which made it all very real and interesting.

**david dalton:** His monologues were hip and out there, almost like Lenny Bruce. He was much hipper than people gave him credit for. He wasn't a manufactured character.

**elvis presley:** In 1956, I met Colonel Sanders…Parker. And they arranged to get me a bunch of chicken! At that particular time, you didn't see people moving too much on television. They were getting it on in the back room. Fourteen years ago it was weird, walking down the street with long hair and sideburns. So I was shakin' and jumpin'. That's how I got into this business… shakin' and jumpin'….I went to Hollywood and made several pictures. I did *Love Me Tender*, *Loving You*, loving her, and several other people I can't tell you about. (Monologue from August 15, 1969 show)

**GEORGE HAMILTON:** Elvis never took himself seriously. He was always very self deprecating. He'd laugh at himself. I remember that night he did a couple of karate chops and he'd start to laugh during one of the sexier moments in his show. It was endearing. People liked this quirkiness in Elvis.

**LAMAR FIKE:** There wasn't much sophistication to Elvis's show. In fact, his shows were famous for their lack of sophistication.

**TERRY BLACKWOOD:** He wasn't the best communicator but he was so stunningly good looking and charismatic. A lot of times you'd mistake the silence between the songs as "Maybe he's not going over well" but it's that people were so captivated by him. He's one of the very few artists I've ever seen who could just mesmerize the crowd just by his good looks, talent and demeanor. He could go from a ballad where he was singing low to a rock and roll song where he was singing above his range. He was a baritone singer and he was hitting notes that a baritone singer should not be able to reach.

**JOE MOSCHEO:** Nobody even noticed any of us onstage. Elvis was so charismatic that when he walked out on stage every eye was on him. Our job was to give him complete attention and our support. We loved being there. He'd look over at us and we'd want to be smiling, we'd want to be alert, we'd want to laugh at the right time and sing at the right time. We were staring at him the entire time and following every move that he made.

**ESTELLE BROWN:** We had to keep an eye on him throughout the show because you never knew what he was gonna do. He was very spontaneous and that kept us on our toes.

**GLEN D. HARDIN:** Elvis was totally unpredictable onstage. He might come up with some old song that nobody had heard for 20 years and he'd simply go right into it.

**JAMES BURTON:** He was the director of the band. He would give you cues. You had to watch him every minute. You couldn't take your eyes off him. It was like working with Jerry Lee Lewis. You'd never know when he'd stop and jump into another song. With Elvis, you had to pick up on all the little things that he was doing. He never did the same thing twice. Every show was different.

**GLEN D. HARDIN:** Not knowing what he was gonna do made it more exciting and fun for us.

**TERRY BLACKWOOD:** I wouldn't consider him a comedian but he was just like a little kid in a toy shop. He'd do things like get a drink of water and whatever he didn't drink he'd throw on Charlie Hodge or he would fall out on the floor lying there on his back. If the microphone didn't work he'd throw it down on the floor. (laughs).

**glen d. hardin:** If you didn't watch Elvis you'd miss something. But if you did watch him he was easy to read.

**joe moscheo:** If he wanted to hear something, we knew by his actions or just a twitch of his mouth what he was looking for and we wanted to give it to him. I think each of the musicians did the same thing. We all had musical ESP. That one hour we were on stage with him, he not only controlled the audience and the dynamics of that performance but he also had total control of the stage.

**myrna smith:** He liked to work off of us and he was so in tune with what we were doing. It seemed he had an ability to hear everything even if we whispered something to one of the band members.

**cissy houston:** Elvis would come over to our side of the stage, pinch you on the arm or say something that would make us laugh. We always had big smiles on our faces working with Elvis. How could you not have a big smile on your face? It was the experience of a lifetime.

**terry blackwood:** Elvis didn't just say, "Hey, look at me." He'd go over to the Sweets or go over to us and he'd interact with us or get affirmation from us during the show. He wanted us to make sure we were included in this event. And of course, with the TCB band too. He knew he had the greatest band money could buy and he wanted to show 'em off.

**james burton:** See, that's the kind of thing we had onstage with Elvis, a lot of energy, excitement, a lot of flash, a lot of great songs, a lot of fast playing and a lot of beautiful ballads. There was no limit to what we could do as a group. Elvis named us the TCB Band. The band had a great chemistry. He needed musicians who could create that same excitement and energy that Elvis created onstage. It couldn't be any other way. He could count on us. We put feeling and soul into everything that we did. It was a perfect marriage between him and the band. We became family, that's the way that Elvis felt about us. He didn't look at us as hired musicians.

**glen d. hardin:** The band worked very well together. Even though we were young, we all had a lot of experience and had grown up with Elvis's music. We really clicked.

**james burton:** His energy affected the way we performed the songs. What was most important was we had to make sure we had the right feel and energy on the songs. When we played the songs onstage, Elvis pushed the tempos up a notch or two. I always enjoyed playing songs like "Mystery Train" and "Tiger Man" because there was a lot of energy and I had a chance to play a lot of the chicken pickin' guitar stuff.

**larry muhoberac:** The backing vocal groups had that same energy and the orchestra players also had their own fire.

**john wilkinson:** We knew exactly what he wanted to hear and how he wanted to hear it. Every night we gave him everything we had and he gave us everything he had.

**cissy houston:** Elvis put all of his energy into his performances and of course we couldn't give anything less. We'd get a feeling from him and then we'd put that feeling into our singing.

**james burton:** Onstage he would key off me on guitar. When we'd play live he was used to hearing a particular lick that was on the record. If I changed it around, he'd look at you and go, "Where's my lick?" (laughs) It was like he was missing something so he had me play a lot of those licks from the records. Being able to put the right lick in the same place was a blessing from God for me.

**marty lacker:** There's a difference between a show drummer and a session drummer. Ronnie Tutt is one of the best show drummers out there. He was the driving force that Elvis loved because he provided him with that bottom and beat. Elvis liked energetic things and Ronnie played the heck out of the drums in the show.

**john wilkinson:** We had a list of songs, and Elvis stuck right to it. In later years, those song lists really didn't mean much. I think many fans saw a completely different Elvis from the one they expected. In the '50s, he would put on a show with his microphone and all that, but by 1969 he changed that in karate moves. That was part of the choreography he wanted. Now, many people may think that his karate chops came naturally, but those were rehearsed. He knew that he was going to put that in the show. He showed us right kicks, left hand kicks, his fists, and he wanted the drums to emphasize his movements. (*Memories: On the Road with Elvis and John Wilkinson*/Peter Verbruggen)

**pat boone:** There wasn't wasn't anybody else who had actually studied karate and could bring some of that into the show. My thought was, "Hey, that doesn't make any sense to do a big karate move at the end of a song" (laughs) and yet it was Elvis and it became a terrific trademark and instantly seemed just right.

**john wilkinson:** As a showman I haven't seen anybody that can match him then or now.

**james burton:** Elvis had a natural born talent. He was not acting onstage. He wasn't copying anybody; he was just doing his thing. It was strange to a lot of people because they'd never seen a singer shake his legs or jump all over the stage. His timing was so good. All of his movements were in time with the rhythm of the song.

**cissy houston:** He was the greatest showman. He danced, he sang, he flirted, and he was bigger than life.

**david dalton:** Much of the audience was the same age as him but they looked a lot older. Time had somehow taken its toll on them but Elvis seemed ageless, almost like a folk hero.

**elvis presley:** People keep telling me I look young. I don't know how I do it, either. I got very heavy at one time when I was in all those movies, but I lose weight very quickly, you know. *(London Evening Standard/ August 2, 1969/Ray Connolly)*

**terry blackwood:** I've worked with a lot of stars in my life. Elvis had a genuine love of people that his fans sensed and they responded to that.

**estelle brown:** The women would go to the edge of the stage and Elvis would lean down to kiss many of them. Sometimes they'd bite his lip and they'd scratch him. They weren't trying to hurt him but they were just so excited. Often the women would get a little too aggressive so security would have to come and pull them off of him.

**lamar fike:** Elvis didn't have a closing song and I told him the perfect song to close the show would be "Can't Help Falling in Love," a song from *Blue Hawaii.*

**cissy houston:** I really connected with "Can't Help Falling in Love" and he sang it so wonderfully, straight from the heart. I'm a singer that loves songs that mean something and I got that from him on that song.

**joe esposito:** That song was always so moving. Whenever I hear that song today I can see him in my mind singing it and know that's what he felt about his fans, just a lot of love.

**ian fraser-thomson:** Elvis thanked the audience for the warm response and he was beaming, smiling ear to ear and basking in his triumph. I don't know if it was sweat or tears coming from his eyes as he launched into "Can't Help Falling in Love".

**cricket mendell coulter:** When the curtain was coming down on that first show, he had a huge grin on his face and his eyes were twinkling. You could tell he knew he had done it. I saw celebrities like Cary Grant and Sammy Davis Jr. standing on their feet and clapping wildly. I'd just seen the show of a lifetime.

**jerry scheff:** Everything went perfectly and we came off the stage in a state of elation. (Elvis Collectors Brasil)

**armond morales:** He felt a great relief that it went so well. But we were all relieved, not just him. The whole team felt like, "Wow, it's gonna be a good month!"

**mac davis:** With that first show, Elvis found himself again. Like the '68 Comeback show, it was a rebirth onstage for Elvis.

**chris hutchins:** That night he had full control of his talent. It was great that he able to go out there and prove it to himself. He chose the songs very carefully and rehearsed very hard. It gave him back a sense of self worth. He lost all his dignity making those films. He told Tom (Jones) that for one of the films he got so fat on purpose because he knew when he'd arrive in Los Angeles they'd give him a few days off to lose weight.

**estelle brown:** He became more self assured because of the response of the crowd. They were throwing things on the stage, they were screaming, they were crying. That helped to build his confidence.

**lamar fike:** He'd hadn't done Vegas since the New Frontier and he bombed there so he didn't know what kind of reaction he'd get. He knew what was on the line and he came through. After he got the first show under his belt he was ready to roll.

**jerry schilling:** He was back in charge of his own game, which he didn't get the opportunity to do in the movies. He didn't have script approval, he didn't have cast approval, and he didn't have director approval. Here in Vegas people couldn't screw around with his music and wouldn't tell him what to do onstage. He knew he had the audience in his hand. He was full of energy. He was back and he was happy.

**t.g. sheppard:** I saw him go into training only two times in his life, for his opening show in Las Vegas in '69 and when he got ready to do the *Aloha from Hawaii* special. Those were the two times I knew of where he really had a goal. His first goal was to come to Las Vegas and set them on their butt and he did.

**maria columbus:** He had something to prove. He wanted to show that he could deliver and claim the city.

**jimmy newman:** Presley hadn't performed for such a long time. Nobody knew what to expect. If we had a concern about Elvis being able to pack the showroom twice a night, after the success of that first show that concern went right out the window. (laughs) All of us at the International Hotel were grinning from ear to ear. We knew Elvis was still the King.

**nicholas naff:** Elvis's first engagement was totally sold out and that established the Presley reputation in Las Vegas.

**bruce banke:** Twenty-eight days later Elvis had broken every Las Vegas attendance record in existence. Over 102,000 fans had an opportunity to see him. His single show record of 2,200 in the 1,500 seat International Showroom will stand forever, thanks to fire department seating limitations that went into effect in the mid-'70s. Seats were so hard to come by that Elvis's fans were happy to sit six or seven people in a booth that was meant for four. A chair in the aisle was almost as good as a seat at ringside. They would have been willing to hang from the chandeliers.

**lamar fike:** It was a perfect room for Elvis because he'd fill it up twice a night. But the bad deal was Colonel set it up for four weeks. That was real rough on Elvis. That was too much for Elvis or any other entertainer. Elton John, Celine Dion and Cher only do one show a night in Vegas.

**ann moses:** The media were bored with his trite movies. If you tuned in a film like *Girls! Girls! Girls!*, it only showed off the smallest amount of his God given talent. After his comeback in Vegas, the media's perception of Elvis drastically changed. He'd proven his legitimacy as an artist.

**t.g. sheppard:** After that first show went so well, the folks at RCA knew that everything in their Elvis catalog was gonna go gold, and if it had already gone gold it would have gone platinum or double platinum. RCA knew Elvis was back with a vengeance.

Opening night, July 31, 1969

# TRIUMPH IN VEGAS: THE POST-SHOW

After the show, spirits were soaring about Elvis's spectacular performance.

**SONNY WEST:** I was over to the side of the stage when he came off and said, "Man, Elvis! Good God! You are something!" He kinda grinned and said, "It felt good." He was ready to go more. He realized this was the start of being back and doing what he really wanted to do.

**JOHN WILKINSON:** We saw him in the dressing room afterwards and he said, "Fellas and singers, we did it! They loved it and we're gonna go do it again." And we said, "You betcha, boss!" He always referred to the show as *our* show, not as his show. You could tell he had a renewed sense of confidence in himself, "Yeah, I'm still viable, I can do this."

**ELVIS PRESLEY:** It gave me a new life. I was human again. There was hope for the future. New things, new ways. It wasn't the same old movies, the same type of songs. I was able to give some feeling, put some expression into my work. And it gave me a chance to do what I do best, sing. (*Los Angeles Herald-Examiner*, Frank Lieberman)

**TERRY BLACKWOOD:** That confidence reflected itself in all his other performances. He was very gratified by the response he got, "Wow, they do like my songs, they do love me!" There were a lot of congratulatory responses after the opening show.

**JAMES BURTON:** Man, after that first show the energy level was so up, I don't think any of us slept for a week.

**ARMOND MORALES:** Elvis was never better than during that opening month in '69. That was him at his peak as a stage performer.

**DAVID STANLEY:** To me, his opening show in Vegas in '69 was the most monumental night in rock and roll because that night he reminded the world that "The King" was back. His charisma, power, and magnetism was like nothing that I'd never seen before or ever seen since.

**JOSEPH KERETA** (elvisnow.com): A woman named Ms. Jay Osaka flew to see Elvis perform in Las Vegas at the International Hotel during his opening engagement in August of 1969. She made arrangements with Colonel Parker's assistant, Tom Diskin, to present Elvis with a gift of a kimono on behalf of his fans in Japan. A meeting was set up in Elvis's suite after the first performance where she presented the kimono to Elvis who was truly touched by this gesture and in returned whispered something to a member of his entourage. When he returned, he gave Elvis a vest and he gave it to Ms. Osaka as a gift. That's an example of what a generous person Elvis was. The vest was designed by I. C. Costume who designed clothing items for Elvis's 1968 TV Special. I'm happy to say that I purchased that brown suede high collar vest and it's now a part of my personal collection.

**FINAL WEEK** — Despite the fact he hasn't made a public appearance in nearly a decade, Elvis Presley has shattered every major showroom attendance record during his current premiere engagement in the International Hotel's, 2,000-seat main showroom.

**pat boone:** We went backstage and he was up and really hyper about the show. I told him how great it was and how excited everything around me was. He saw my daughter, Debby and he couldn't believe she was now in her early teens. He remembered her as a little tyke who used to jump up and get him wet out by the pool at our home in Bel-Air. Meeting with him backstage you could feel his sense of relief and exultation that he had truly pulled it off. By the time he opened he'd had tremendous sales and people were flying in from around the world. So they knew it would be a success for the hotel but of course he wanted the personal success of deserving the adulation. He knew he needed to create the excitement, which of course he was so good at.

**carol channing:** I went to the reception after the show and he joked when he saw me, "Ain't you in show business?" (laughs) He was darling.

**patti parry:** Backstage, Cary Grant had tears in his eyes and said "I've never seen a show like that." Elvis was thrilled by that.

**bobby vinton:** After the show I went backstage and congratulated Elvis on a great show. My agent asked, "Could Bobby and Elvis have a picture together?" Colonel kind of gave him a look like he wasn't supposed to ask for that. I remember Colonel saying, I don't really let Elvis take pictures with too many other singers. There's only a few that I would do that with." Elvis said, "No come on, let's do it." I remember he put his arm around me and we took the photo. It was really exciting.

**steve binder:** I tried to go backstage to see Elvis after the show but I could never get through the entourage. I was persona non grata after the '68 special because I got too close to Elvis, just like D.J. (Fontana) and Scotty (Moore). The Colonel perceived us as threats to his relationship. I'm convinced beyond a shadow of a doubt that Colonel Parker said, "No Binder in your life from here on out."

**joe esposito:** Once he got the feeling they still loved his music he couldn't wait to get back out on that stage. He had all the confidence in the world and had a ball after that. But he was always nervous before he walked on stage before every show. But once he got out there and kicked off the first song, he was back on track and the nerves went away.

**chris hutchins:** That show was an absolute high point. He was in great form. Joe (Esposito) told me afterwards that he didn't go to bed at all that night. He was just so excited.

**david stanley:** I remember going backstage after the show and looked at Elvis and said, "That was unbelievable!" Elvis looked at me and said, "David, I've been wrong for so long but tonight I'm right." Vernon embraced Elvis and there was that moment of, Wow, my concert career just started again. Vernon, Dee, Priscilla, my brothers and I all felt so much pride after that show. We all felt, "My God, this guy just knocked it out of the park!"

**sonny west:** We were backstage talking about how great the show was and all of sudden here comes Colonel Parker into the room and he looked very emotional.

**loanne miller parker:** The Colonel was thrilled at the reception Elvis got because he wanted this for Elvis so badly. For him to see Elvis triumph like that just blew his mind. He was so proud.

**sonny west:** He quietly asked, "Where is he?" We told him that he was changing and he kind of nodded and just stood there and didn't move. A couple of minutes later the doors opened up and Elvis came out. Elvis turned and he saw Colonel and the Colonel went up to him and hugged him with tears in his eyes.

**bruce banke:** Colonel was weeping and saying, "We did it. We did it."

**sonny west:** And Elvis said, "Yeah, we did Colonel, we did."

**joe esposito:** Colonel Parker's a tough man but he was emotional that night. It touched Elvis.

**sonny west:** This was the only time I ever saw something like this.

**bruce banke:** Colonel grew up in an era when men didn't show emotion or cry as either was considered a weakness. Knowing that in show business only the strong survive, he was careful not to let his guard down. Rarely did anyone see him in an emotional moment. He saved those for only those closest to him.

**loanne miller parker:** The Colonel had a very tough exterior because inside he was a very soft person. He always feared people would take advantage of that. Because of that he showed a very tough exterior to the world. People depended on him to be strong and steady and he didn't let us down.

**sonny west:** Then all of sudden the Colonel was back to being the Colonel. "Joe, Sonny, I need him up there for the press conference." And just like that, we were back to business again.

# elvis speaks: the press conference

Following Elvis's triumphant comeback show, sometime after midnight on August 1, 1969, a gathering of international media were assembled. Into a ballroom sauntered a victorious Elvis dressed all in black except for a fiery red and black scarf wrapped around his neck. Colonel Tom Parker announced, "This will be the last press party you will ever see." Standing behind a table flanked by his father, Vernon, and members of the Memphis Mafia, Elvis fielded questions from the media. After the short press conference was over, Elvis freely mingled with the press, giving out autographs and taking photos. Rock and roll legend Fats Domino and comedian Rodney Dangerfield were among the celebs in attendance photographed with Presley.

**bruce banke:** Midway through Elvis's single opening night performance Colonel decided to hold a press conference after the show and asked the publicity department to set it up.

**ANN MOSES:** I remember getting a tap on the shoulder and someone told me, "There's gonna be a press conference."

**bruce banke:** This was a surprise decision that had the hotel's catering staff scurrying to set up a press interview area complete with a head table and sound system in a room located inside the hotel's 70,000 square-foot Grand Ballroom.

**MYRAM borders:** The tradition in Las Vegas is that the media would be invited backstage into the dressing room to interview the star. Well, in this case, there was too much press there to accommodate everyone so they couldn't do that. The media were requesting interviews with Elvis and that was the only way they could accommodate them without irritating any other members of the media who didn't get an interview. So they held one big mass press conference.

**ian Fraser-thomson:** After the show concluded, and as people were filing out, I was busy collecting memorabilia and the invitational menus from the tables. Someone in front of the stage said, "Hey Pat, are you going backstage to see Elvis?" I turned around and saw Pat Boone, who was there with his daughter Debby. He said he'd already seen Elvis before the show and mentioned he was doing a press conference. The guy said, "Yeah, it's gonna be in the convention room." I went, "Oh my God, there's a press conference going on?" I found out from a security guard where the convention room was. I went into the gift shop and got myself a pen. I was thinking, what in the world can I say to get into this press conference? I thought maybe I'll say I'm from AP (Associated Press) or UPI (United Press International). There was no one at the door so I loosened my tie and just walked in.

**MARIA COLUMBUS:** We had a fan club, "The Elvis Special", and we tried to see if there would be a press conference following Elvis's opening show. I sent a letter to the International Hotel and got a letter back from Nick Naff, the International Hotel's publicity director. In the letter he said they'd contact us if there was a press conference but we never heard anything. My friend, Jeannie Tessum, and I went out to Vegas for Elvis's first show and I brought the letter with me. We ran into the Colonel outside the showroom during the afternoon and showed him the letter. He said, "There is a press conference and I'll get you both in." He signed the letter and said to show it to the guard at the door to gain entry into the press conference. We got there and the guard said, "I can't let you in, this is for the press only." Colonel Parker must have been watching out for us because he came out, took our arms and walked us in. The guard's jaw hit the floor, he was shocked.

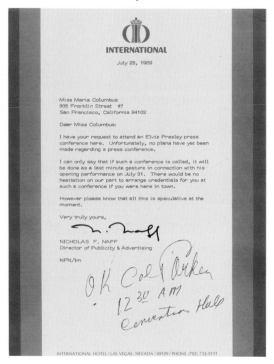

**BRUCE BANKE:** They expected 200 writers and photographers to attend. Members of the press were thrilled with the opportunity to talk to the King and thanked the Colonel profusely. The real reason for the press conference, however, wasn't meant to enlighten the media or give them rare photo opportunities, although it did accomplish that. Colonel knew that many of them were headed out to midnight shows at competing hotels featuring other Las Vegas headliners. By keeping them tied up at a press conference for a couple of hours, they wouldn't be able to make the shows and, thereby, write about any entertainer other than Elvis the next day.

**JOE ESPOSITO:** Elvis walked in with a big huge smile on his face and he never looked better in his life.

**IAN FRASER-THOMSON:** As soon as he came in the room exploded in cheers.

**MARIA COLUMBUS:** All of the media stood up and gave him a standing ovation and I think Elvis was really surprised. You could tell that the media was completely blown away by his show.

**SONNY WEST:** He was so happy and excited because of how well the show had gone but he had to keep himself cool up there and keep a rein on his emotions because if he didn't he would have been acting like a 10-year-old kid in a candy store.

**bruce banke:** The press conference was a Colonel classic. He wore his traditional white floor length smock emblazoned with ELVIS! IN PERSON! INTERNATIONAL HOTEL! all over it. He stood off to the side and let Elvis field the questions.

**t.g. sheppard:** Elvis knew how to work the media, he was the master. He knew how to get what he wanted and he knew how to give them what they wanted.

**ann moses:** He was really comfortable with the media because he was still so fired up from that show. Any lack of self confidence was gone after that show. He knew he had nailed it.

**bruce banke:** The mood was very relaxed as Elvis stood in front of the podium, one foot planted on an adjacent chair and surrounded by his father and friends. He knew the show had been a resounding success and he was enjoying every minute of it.

**ian fraser-thomson:** Elvis remained standing and took questions. He was in a jubilant mood and was very animated. He was very humble and appreciative of all the attention. At the press conference I got a small sample of Elvis the man. No star attitude, a quiet humility was evident in this man called "The King".

**chris hutchins:** It was mainly American journalists, the writers I brought out from London and a couple of Japanese media. Elvis was very polite. The press didn't ask any real tough questions.

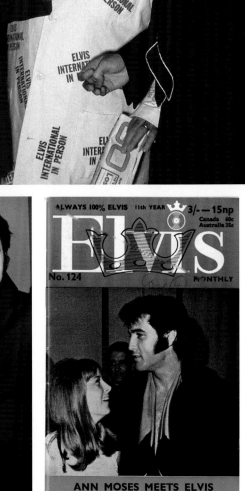

**rodney bingenheimer:** Elvis talked about how he wanted to change his movie image—he said it was getting harder and harder to perform in front of a movie camera. He also talked about how teenagers were changing for the better.

**bruce banke:** The verbal exchange between the media and the star was fast paced. Elvis was having fun, the writers were eating it up, cameras were flashing everywhere and the Colonel stood on the sidelines, smoking his cigar and smiling contentedly.

ALWAYS 100% ELVIS  11th YEAR  **3/- — 15np**  Canada 60c  Australia 35c

# ELVIS

No. 124                    MONTHLY

**ANN MOSES MEETS ELVIS**

## PRESS CONFERENCE (selected excerpts):

**Why have you waited so long to perform live again?**
We had to finish up the movie commitments before I could start on this.

**How did it feel being back in front of a live audience after so many years?**
Fantastic. I really missed it. I love the live contact with an audience. It was getting harder and harder to perform to a movie camera all day long. The inspiration wasn't there. I'm tired of playing a guy singing to the guy he's beating up.

**Did you enjoy performing live again?**
Yes! This has been one of the most exciting nights of my life.

**Did you feel nervous during the show?**
For the first three songs or so, before I loosened up. Then I thought, "What the heck. Get with it, man, or you might be out of a job tomorrow."

**Were you a little afraid onstage tonight?**
Yes, I was at first, until I got going, and then I felt okay. I was nervous and didn't feel relaxed until after "Love Me Tender."

**How did you choose the songs for your show?**
I just sang my favorites, that's all.

**Do you want to do more live shows?**
I want to...I would like to play all over the world. I chose Las Vegas to play first because it is a place people come to from all over.

**Do you like leather jackets like the one you wore on your TV specials?**
No. I hate wearing leather jackets because they are just too hot to work in.

**Why did you choose a Negro backup group (The Sweet Inspirations)?**
Because they help to give me my feel, my soul.

**Where did you get the idea for your stage outfit?**
I got the idea from a karate gi I once had.

**Do you dye your hair?**
Sure, because I've always done it for the movies.

**Why do you dye your hair?**
Because it's gray.

**Why do you choose to record message type songs like "In the Ghetto"? Are you trying to change your image?**
No. "Ghetto" was such a great song. I just couldn't pass it up after I'd heard it. There are a lot of new records out now that have the same sound I started but they're better. I mean, you can't compare a song like "Yesterday" with "Hound Dog", can you?

**How do you feel about the Hollywood social scene?**
I just don't go for it. I have nothing against it but I just don't enjoy it.

**Why have you led such a secluded life all these years?**
It's not secluded, honey. I'm just sneaky.

**How long did you rehearse for these shows?**
I practiced for nearly three months. Today I went through three complete dress rehearsals. This was the fourth time I did that show today. I'm really beat.

**Can you remember the first time you were in Las Vegas?**
Sure, I was 19 years old. Nobody knew me. "Where you from, boy?" they'd ask.

**Will you be back in Las Vegas soon?**
Absolutely. I love Las Vegas because it attracts people from all over the world.

**Do you have a share in the International Hotel?**
No, I have not.

**Are you tired of your present type of movie?**
Yes. I want to change the type of scripts I have been doing.

**What kind of scripts do you like?**
Something with meaning. I'm going after more serious material. I couldn't dig always playing the guy who'd get into a fight, beat the guy up, and in the next shot sing to him.

**Do you feel it was a mistake to do so many soundtrack albums?**
I think so. When you do ten songs in a movie, they can't all be good songs.

**Will you be doing any more movies?**
I don't know. I kinda got tired of beating up guys and then having to sing a song to them or maybe their horses.

**Mr. Presley, I've been sent here by Lord Sutch Enterprises to offer you one million pounds sterling to make two appearances at the Wembley Empire Stadium in England. This price will include a documentary that will be filmed during and after the shows. It will only take 24 hours.**
You'll have to ask him about that. (Elvis points to Colonel Parker) Colonel Parker: Make an offer! Cash, not pounds! Just put down the deposit.

**How much do you get paid for these performances?**
Colonel Parker: We are pleased with the deal. I am glad he is here.

**Would you like to appear in England?**
I definitely would like to appear in England as we have had so many requests. And it will be soon, as we are now doing live concerts again.

**Is there any truth to the rumor that you are getting a slice of the hotel as part of the fee?**
Colonel Parker: Certainly not. The only thing we got free were crickets in the room.

**Have you still got about 10 cars?**
I never had that many, only four or five at the most.

**After all this time you look so young.**
I guess I'm just lucky. I really don't know. I guess one of these days it will catch up with me and I'll probably fall apart.

**Have you ever seen England's top pop singer Cliff Richard?**
Yes, I met him in Germany a long time ago.

**How does it feel to be a father?**
Great. I love it!

**Do you and Priscilla plan to add to your family?**
We'll have to wait and see.

**How does Priscilla feel about you being such a great sex symbol?**
I don't know... you would have to ask her.

**Are you planning to have any more kids?**
Yes, we are planning to add to our family. Thank you very much.

**Is there any other individual you would rather be?**
Are you kidding?

**What's it like to be the Grandfather of rock and roll?**
(laughs) I didn't know that I was.

**Are you doing shows because of the recent success of Tom Jones in cabaret?**
No, that's not the reason. Although I admire Tom Jones very much, and think he's a great talent. I guess I felt it was time to do live shows because I missed doing them.

**I noticed in your repertoire you did some Beatle songs. What do you think of the Beatles and their material?**
I admire the Beatles and think they are very good. The lyrics of pop songs are getting better all the time, they have more meaning.

**When you met the Beatles, why was there no press allowed?**
I guess it was because we could relax and talk friendly to each other.

**Did anyone influence you in your career?**
Yes, people like him. (Elvis introduces Fats Domino) This is one of my influences from way back, Fats Domino. Just look at those rings and that diamond watch, aren't they fabulous?

**FATS DOMINO:** I was so impressed with him. His personality was so nice and he was wonderful to talk to. Not only was he the nicest entertainer I ever met but he was also one of the nicest gentlemen I've ever met. If you met him you'd love him too. I know that I did. I still think about him all the time.

**MARIA COLUMBUS:** Colonel Parker stopped the press conference after 20 minutes.

**IAN FRASER-THOMSON:** The Colonel said, "Ladies and gentlemen, sitting here on the table are some press packages, which you're welcome to. They have some photographs of Elvis and if you want to you can come up and get an autograph from Elvis."

**MARIA COLUMBUS:** Then he jokingly said, "And there'll be no extra charge for that." (laughs) The press just rushed forward and surrounded him. But Elvis was patient with the media and talked to everybody.

**IAN FRASER-THOMSON:** I raced up to the table, grabbed a press package and went through the line and had Elvis sign an 8x10. I immediately went back into the line and ultimately did that three times. The last time Elvis recognized me and asked my name and signed a photo, "To Ian, Elvis Presley." Then I asked him a question about a song I really liked from *Viva Las Vegas.* I said, "Elvis what do you think about 'I Need Somebody to Lean On'?" It was a melancholy favorite of mine that touched me very much. Elvis had a curious look on his face and said, "That was a ballad, wasn't it?" Right after he said that a voice from the back of the room voice bellowed out, "Hey Elvis!" Elvis turned to look at him and said, "Hey Fats!" and of course it was Fats Domino. Then he put his hand up to hold Fats Domino off and he looked back at me and said, "Did I answer your question?" I thought, wow, that was a really polite and respectful thing to do. And I went, "Yeah Elvis, you answered the question." I was formulating lots of other things I wanted to talk to him about but by that time Fats Domino was taking front stage there. Anyhow, then Elvis said, "Hey, can I have your pen?" I feel bad about this now but I said no. I said, "No Elvis, I want to get an autograph from your dad" and he just said, "Okay," I had Vernon sign a photo and as he was signing it I said, "You must be very proud of your son" (imitates southern accent), "Well yes I am."

**rodney bingenheimer:** After the press conference was over we were invited up to meet him. He was very friendly and in great spirits. I met him and got him to sign my menu. In fact, there's a picture of him signing my menu. I showed Elvis's dad, Vernon a photo of Elvis from a contact sheet that I kept in my wallet. He looked at the photo and pointed at the sweater Elvis was wearing and said, "I gave that sweater to Elvis."

**maria columbus:** When Elvis was talking to other people we noticed he was wearing a jacket with no shirt and a multi-colored silk scarf. Jeannie and I always debated after seeing those promotional photos of Elvis shirtless from *Blue Hawaii* that it looked like he had no hair on his chest. So while Elvis was talking in front of us, I turned to Jeannie and said, "He does have his hair on his chest." Elvis stopped his conversation, turned to me and said, "Yes honey I do." and he laughed. Then he turned back and continued talking to some other people. I was shocked and also mortified that he heard me say that. I remember there was a very pretty statuesque blonde showgirl who wore a very low cut dress and Elvis put a carnation down her cleavage. Everybody laughed and thought it was very funny.

# victory: the post show celebration

**sonny west:** After the first show he felt rejuvenated. He wanted to be a good actor and he was. But playing live was what got him going and he was excited to be back.

**bobby morris:** We celebrated in his suite on the 30th floor. Elvis was so happy and relieved the show had gone so well.

**joe esposito:** The suite on top of the hotel where Elvis stayed was the biggest suite in Las Vegas and probably around the world. It was a four bedroom suite that was over 10,000 square feet and that was a lot of square footage in those days.

**bobby morris:** All glass. That suite was beyond belief. Beautiful views.

**joe esposito:** There was a huge patio outside overlooking the city.

**loanne miller parker:** Half of that floor was a bar called the Crown Room. The walls on that floor were made of glass and you could look out and see the whole city. At night Las Vegas was magic. On a cloudy night there were so many marquees lit up that it reflected against the clouds and you'd swear it was daylight.

**t.g. sheppard:** It was quite a celebration. Everybody was on such a high. Elvis could relax now. Every show after that was like a piece of cake.

# talk of the town

Elvis's return to the stage was big news around the world, generating massive press coverage among the international media.

Joe Delaney
*Las Vegas Sun*
August 1, 1969

Elvis Presley made his first public stage appearance anywhere in eight years last night when he opened a four week engagement at the International Hotel...It is 13 years since Elvis worked LV. His previous and only appearance in our town was at the old Frontier Hotel on a bill headlined by Shecky Greene...We predict that Elvis will have his more enthusiastic followers walking around asking, "Tom Who?" and "Engelbert Who?" when comparison are attempted. Streisand's record at the International will be broken...Elvis represents the finest effort by that master promoter, Colonel Tom Parker. Of course, the "product" was there. If not, it would have been just one around. Elvis is very much for real. Elvis is here to stay.

Ray Connolly
*London Evening Standard*
August 2, 1969

Elvis Presley came back from celluloid wilderness of Hollywood over the weekend to make his first public appearance in nine years. For a reputed fee of £225,000 the god of rock and roll returned to the stage in a blaze of advertising at the brand new International Hotel in this hot and lunatic town of Las Vegas. I've already seen the show three times and I can tell you he is sensational - better than any of us could ever have imagined. Twice nightly for 28 days he will be appearing for the rich and their womenfolk. "It is," he says, "the most exciting thing I've done in years." But it was the first appearance on the first night that had all the drama. He was out of this world, better by far than I - always the greatest Presley fan in world - could possibly have hoped for, and a lesson in himself to the entertainment media of our generation. For a full hour he worked and sweated, gyrated and shuddered, warbled and sang, and grunted and groaned his way through 20 songs. It was a sensational comeback. Looking as slim as a ramrod, and not a day over 23 (he's actually 34 now), he ambled back on to the stage after a nine year absence like a sheepish young lad going to meet his girl friend's parents for the first time. Hardly daring to look or acknowledge the audience, which was composed mainly of over-thirties, since young people could never normally afford the price, he went straight into "Blue Suede Shoes" and had completed "I Got A Woman" and "That's All Right, Mama" before finding it necessary to begin any chatting. For over an hour he flogged himself to near exhaustion moving wildly and sexily around the stage all the time, and now and again reaching for a handkerchief or a glove from the ecstatic and many-splendored ladies in the front row...It was indeed a memorable night. The night when Elvis Presley, the founder of much of modern day pop music, discovered that he is still one of greatest performers and went back to doing what he always did best.

Myram Borders
*Nevada State Journal*
August 5, 1969

Swivel-hipped singer Elvis Presley broke all attendance records on the "Strip" during the first seven days of a month long engagement. About 125 persons were lined up at the showroom reservation counter early Monday, normally a slow day. Last Saturday some 500 persons were there at 10 A.M. in hopes of getting reservations during the busy weekend. Many were turned away. Officials at the International Hotel said weekends were sold out and that bookings during the week were "tight" for Presley's first appearance before a live audience in eight years. Some Presley fans came all the way from Europe to see the show.

The hotel received a letter from a woman in France with a 100 franc note enclosed as a deposit for 10 shows. The woman wanted reservations for both the dinner and midnight shows for five straight days. "So far we have yet to have an empty seat in the house. He is the hottest thing that has hit Las Vegas," said Bruce Banke, an executive of the hotel. It was his first stage appearance in eight years and his only return engagement to Las Vegas in 13 years. Presley in the flesh has lost nothing. It was still all there. Gyrating legs... wide stance ... a bobbing head with tossed black hair ... rotating guitar ...knee bends and the pounding rhythm of such tunes as "Blue Suede Shoes," "Hound Dog," "Jailhouse Rock," "Heartbreak Hotel" and one of his newest recordings "In The Ghetto".

He was contracted to appear here for an undisclosed salary. "We are very happy with the deal." said Col. Tom Parker, the distinguished Presley manager with the honorary southern title. He blithely side-stepped the question of how much the performance was costing the International Hotel. Reportedly, Presley is being paid as much as Barbra Streisand who opened the resort in early July for a reported $1 million during a three-year period. Parker has deftly guided Presley, the Tennessee country boy, to the top of the heap in money earnings. Presley has recorded almost 50 gold records, an unprecedented number, and has made millions in movies.

Presley arrived in Las Vegas a week before the July 31 opening and practiced daily. He still was rehearsing at 5 P.M. on opening night—two hours before the invited guests began arriving. Actor George Hamilton was among the first nighters along with performers such as Carol Channing and businessmen of the Howard Hughes organization. A plane load of admirers flew in from Atlanta, and members of the news media converged here from the East Coast and Europe. Temperatures outside the International Hotel neared 110 degrees the night Presley opened inside the 2,000 seat showroom - after viewing an hour of Presley's gyrations—blood pressure were on the rise. "Oh... it's Elvis," walled a woman in her fifties as if she were surprised to see the star after fighting long lines for hours to get a seat. Presley received a long standing ovation. It was one of the rare occasions when a Las Vegas standing salute was sincere rather than rigged with a few cronies of an entertainer planted down front to stamp and scream approval.

MYRAM BORDERS (writer, *Nevada State Journal*): When Elvis first played in Vegas in '56 there was still somewhat of a prudish attitude going on. He'd been criticized a lot by Middle America over his hip movements and they asserted that he was the devil of a new fangled kind of music that was gonna lead all the kids astray. That attitude had disappeared by the time he returned in '69. First of all, they'd heard a lot more about Elvis in all the years that interceded. He was a name by the time he came back. When he was here in the '50s I don't think he was a star, he was a controversial entertainer.

There was a lot of excitement in town about Elvis's opening. The show was really hyped with every kind of publicity you can think of. His performance certainly was energized. It didn't show that he was under a great deal of pressure or nervous, it showed that he was a hell of an entertainer in full command of his abilities. There was nothing quite like Elvis's body movements and he certainly had a great voice. He had it all together that night as he did for a long time while he was in Vegas. At the end of his show, Elvis received a standing ovation from the audience and it wasn't one of the phony ones. Sometimes an entertainer would receive a standing ovation because they had plants in the first couple of rows who would stand up and the crowd eventually would stand up. But Elvis earned his standing ovation. The audience literally leapt to its feet at the end of the show. The feedback from the media in attendance was that they'd seen the return of a great entertainer.

*Variety*
August 6, 1969

The Elvis Presley who was a freakish kid curiosity when he was third-billed on a New Frontier showbill in 1956 is no more. He has become "ELVIS," not only in huge electric letters on the International's marquee, but in most publicized and verbalized affirmations of his superstar status...Presley took all things in fine stride at the preem, with most star acts on the Strip in attendance and a total of about 2,000 present. No verbal hurrah or musical fanfare accompanied his slouching, grinning amble from the wings, dressed in open-neck black blouse and bell trousers. He was immediately affable and, although nervous, very much in command of the entire scene as he went on to prove himself as one of the more potent Vegas lures.

James D. Kingsley
*Billboard*
August 9, 1969

The greatest rocker of them all came and met one of his toughest audiences at the International Hotel showroom...It was probably Elvis' toughest challenge since he rocked out of the South with long sideburns, rotating pelvis and a banged up guitar...But it was not the Elvis with the rough edges of the middle 1950s, on stage Thursday. It was a polished, confident and talented artist, knowing exactly what he was going to do and when. But it was the Elvis of the past as he "Put the feeling into the songs, and let the vibrations of the music have their say, swinging hips, revolving pelvis and moving shoulders."

*Record Mirror*
August 9, 1969

The swivel hips of the greatest rock and roller in history swung again on Thursday, July 31 after seven years without a wiggle. Elvis Presley leapt on stage at America's gigantic International Hotel showroom, lifting the mike like a hot bull whip and swiftly reinstated himself as one of the most polished performers of all time. Since long before the invitation-only opening night performance, seething Las Vegas has been alight with signs proclaiming the return of the King and all shows through August 28 have been booked solid…It was a young night as Presley, like a wild beast, roared through a long list of the songs that made him famous. "Hound Dog," "Don't Be Cruel," "One Night," "Blue Suede Shoes" and many more brought him massive ovations and closed the long gap that had frustrated rockers the world over. His strenuous gyrations and virile voicing caused a tumult of uproar from the screaming patronage as ladies lost years and threw themselves at the feet of their leader in frenzied glory. The King jerked and twisted, coaxing the response from the audience. He had to be sure it was all right. There was confidence in every drop of sweat that rolled down his face, but he had to hear it from them—- and they told him. Better and more powerful than ever before, Elvis had reunited fans with their idol; a movement with its leader…Over 12,000 fans have already paid up to £20 a ticket to see the first six shows and there is 80% of capacity reserved for the remainder of the season. Pat O'Neill, of the publicity staff, said, "It is one of the biggest advance reservations requests I have ever heard of."…Married and with a family, Elvis has shown that nothing was lost in the years he spent in the background. If anything, his ghostly absence has served more to heighten expectation for his new arrival and the reception clearly demonstrates that the young lion has been unleashed with twice the power and luster of the legendary teenager from the South with the unruly sideboards and the beat-up guitar.

Michael Ross
*Los Angeles Herald-Examiner*
August 12, 1969

His victims are now 30-plus. Hardened waitresses, who just recently struggled through the ennuied debut of The Divine Barbra, were visibly swooning. A well-attired matron scrambled on stage without breaking stride and corralled the shy Presley. And his artistry is undiminished. In fact, he seems even enhanced when compared to the rather trendy impulse by some "to return to the roots of rock 'n roll." When Elvis swings into "Blue Suede Shoes" and "I Got a Woman" and "All Shook Up," and all the others, he is where it is at. That's one of the few truths in pop music.

Rodney Bingenheimer
*GO* magazine
August 1969

It was one of the most memorable events in my life. I attended the opening of Elvis Presley at the International Hotel in Las Vegas, along with Lord Sutch. We missed the first plane and had to catch the next one. We got there just in time. We got off the plane in 119 degree heat. Hot, hot, hot!...We took a cab straight to the hotel and were greeted by Nick Naff and we were seated third table from the front. We were lucky to get that close...Looking unbelievable young, dressed in a black suit with a sash around it, long black hair and side-burns, he immediately went into "Blue Suede Shoes." You could tell that he was a little scared. Then he did "I Got a Woman," dancing around doing the steps that a lot of top singers have copied from him. He did "That's All Right," the first record he ever recorded. He did the lovely ballad "Love Me Tender," and went into a medley of his RCA hits, "Jailhouse Rock," "Don't Be Cruel," "Heart-break Hotel," (doing that one like he did in '56), "All Shook Up," "Hound Dog," and he really freaked out in "Hound Dog." He really got out of breath during most of the numbers. Elvis said, "It's the first time I've worked in front of people for nine years, and it may be my last...I don't know." He also did "Memories," My Babe," I Can't Stop Loving You," "In the Ghetto," and a new one called "Suspicious Minds," which he recorded in Memphis. He also did Lennon and McCartney's "Yesterday" and went into sixteen bars of "Hey Jude." He also did "Johnny B. Goode," "Mystery Train," "Tiger Man" and What I'd Say." What a showman! Of course he got a standing ovation and an encore! He came back with "Can't Help Falling in Love." ....His dynamic stage performance shows why he is admired and imitated by many of today's top names in the music world....Elvis is still the king of rock and roll and a great showman of our times.

Mike Jahn
*New York Times*
August 18, 1969

Elvis Presley, the "old groaner" of the rock 'n' roll generation, still has his snarl. The acknowl-edged king of early rock opened a month's engagement at the immense new International Hotel here and had everyone shaking their heads in wonder....With all this time away from an audience, it would be logical to expect him to rust a bit. With his stature, it is fairly logical to expect him to go the Vegas route, that is, live out the rest of his life singing soft ballads in the style of Dean Martin or Paul Anka...The Vegas route is the easy way, and it was expected that this is what Presley would do. But, with the opening song on his first night, it was clear that Elvis Presley still knows how to sing rock 'n' roll. He seems, in fact, to have lost nothing in the past decade...Elvis Presley came to this place and provided an unbelievable exercise in pure, exciting rock 'n' roll. Despite the flashiness, despite the fact that most of the male customers had awful James Bond fixations and most all the women seemed to dress out of the Fredericks of Hollywood catalogue (see it sometime, it's cheaper than Myron Cohen), Elvis Presley made Las Vegas an incredible experience.

**mike jahn** (writer, *New York Times*): I was the first full-time rock critic for any major publication. I was a big Elvis fan when I was a teenager; I loved his Sun Records stuff and some of the early RCA stuff. I didn't like the music that he did after he came out of the army. I thought that it was overproduced and schmaltzy. He'd been doing all those shitty movies. I thought if he didn't change things he'd wind up doing those movies for the rest of his life and wind up being married to Ann-Margret and living somewhere in Beverly Hills with a heart shaped pool in the backyard. To me he was going the direction of all performers when they get older, eventually they're gonna be in Vegas and I saw that coming for Elvis. So I flew out to the opening of Elvis's Vegas come-back shows with my first wife, Carol. At the time Vegas was scummy and sleazy. It was like the old Times Square in New York City. It was run down, full of hookers and really dirty. It was not a fun place. I hated it. But today I love Vegas. Now it's like a theme park.

There was a party ahead of time for him and some guy came over and said, "Do you want to meet Elvis?" He was standing only about ten feet away shaking hands with some people. But I said, "No, why would I want to meet Elvis Presley? He's just a washed up singer from the '50s who's now starting his career as a Vegas lounge act." So my expectations for his show were low. In my mind he was a has been who was great in his own time. Also, by that point, he was viewed within the media more as a curiosity and less as a legitimate artist.

Anyway, we were escorted to our table and sat with a bunch of VIPs. We were sitting right across from Henry Mancini. Then Elvis came out and he was sensational. It wasn't a watered down stage act. He really went out there and rocked. He was not going through the motions. I was astonished. I think he was even been better than he was in the '50s. I said to myself, "Holy shit, I should have tried to meet him!" (laughs) I was completely blown away. That night he proved that he was anything but a has been. It was also an important event for me on a personal level because that's where we conceived our son.

Ellen Willis
*The New Yorker*
August 30, 1969

Presley came on and immediately shook up all my expectations and preconceived categories. There was a new man out there. A grown man in black bell-bottoms, tunic, and neckerchief, devoid of pout and baby fat, skinny, sexy, totally alert, nervous but smiling easily…He still moved around a lot but in a much different spirit. What was once deadly-serious frenzy had been infused with humor and a certain detachment: This is where it began—isn't it a good thing? Though the show was more than anything else an affirmation of Presley's sustaining love for rhythm and blues—we knew it all the time, Elvis—it was not burdened by an oppressive reverence for the past. He knew better than to try to be nineteen again. He had quite enough to offer at thirty-three.

David Dalton
*Rolling Stone*
February 21, 1970

Elvis was Supernatural, his own resurrection, at the Showroom International in Las Vegas last August. Everyone complained that Las Vegas was a bad choice, but you only have to look at the old color publicity photos of Elvis to know why it was the only possible place for him to make his debut after nine years of hibernation: The iconic, frontal image, completely symmetrical, stares out of the glossy blue background. The glaring eyes, the surly mouth, the texture of the face completely airbrushed out, the hair jet black with blue metallic streaks – these are superhuman attributes. It is the disembodied face of Krishna, Christ, Mao, where the image dominates the reality. The adherence to this formula has been so dogmatic that until recently you were in danger of a lawsuit from the Colonel if you used a photo of Elvis that was not the officially-sanctioned publicity handout...Even Elvis seemed to find his reincarnation hard to believe. Mumbling, "Whass that, whass that?" He suddenly interrupted one of his long monologues like a speed flash—"Oh, it's okay, it's me, it's me!" And it was hard to believe as the curtain finally went up for the third time on Elvis. His head hung down, legs braced for his defiant stance and an acoustic guitar symbolically slung around his neck.

 Elvis is wearing a blue karate jump suit with a long karate belt. His bellbottoms have bright red satin vents and he's wearing a red and white scarf around his neck. His black pointed boots have studs on the toes and heels. His hair is cut in a short Beatle fringe at the front but he's still wearing the Presley sideburns. Behind him is a six-piece band from Memphis and behind them a twenty-five piece orchestra silhouetted by glowing backdrop lighting that oozes through a syrupy range of chartreuse, cerise and aquamarine. To his right are the Sweet Inspirations, a soul group that preceded him with some insipid versions of show tunes. Behind them, Elvis's own back-up group, the Imperials, neatly dressed in blazers.

 Elvis speaks. "Viva Las Vegas," he says, laughing; "No, man, that's one man, that's one number I ain't gonna do" —unexpectedly revealing his attitude to the twelve years of schlock movies. "Welcome to the Showroom Internationale, ladies and gentlemen. This is somethin' else, ain't it? Lookin' 'round at all them decorations, funky angels hangin' from the ceilin'... tell ya there ain't nothin' like a funky angel, boy."

 Presiding over the gigantic dining room and its 2,000 paying guests are a giant 20-foot pair of paper maché statues representing Marie Antoinette and Louis XIV, holding a lace handkerchief the size of a tablecloth, and from the ceiling hangs a pair of gargantuan cherubs exchanging a length of cream satin material. Above the stage there's a dumpy coat of arms, strictly from Walt Disney. Funky.

 Elvis's backing band is tight and probably a lot better as musicians than Bill Black and Scotty Moore, who played on Elvis' early disks, but the sound is bland and professional. The arrangements, too, are more stylized than the originals. The drumming, for instance, is very syncopated, especially in the fast numbers, imitating the percussive hiccupping quality of Elvis' voice in songs like 'All Shook Up' ("I'm in love" – boom boom boom)....

 After a pause to catch his breath, Elvis modestly mumbles, "This is my first personal appearance in nine years." Thunderous applause, and from the balcony a couple of kids are shouting, "Dynamite, baby, too much." But the audience is super-straight, mostly middle-aged people with children and affluent old Elvis fans in their late thirties, their ducktails trimmed into neat executive crew cuts, their leather jackets turned in for seersucker suits...

 As an encore he does his 1962 hit "Can't Help Falling in Love." "You've been a beautiful audience, ladies and gentlemen, you've made it all worthwhile."

 As we are walking out into the casino, a balding man with a beer belly is handing out thirteen-year-old color photos of Elvis. Someone says, "Hey man, you know who that is? It's Colonel Parker."

**bRuce bANke** (assistant director of publicity and advertising, International Hotel):
A headline in *Billboard* magazine read, "Elvis Retains Touch in Return to Stage." Around the world the reviews were glowing. One would have thought the Colonel had written them himself.

# ELVIS DRAWS 101,500 IN 4-WEEK HOTEL RUN

LAS VEGAS (℗—Elvis Presley, making his first Las Vegas appearance in 13 years, drew 101,500 persons in four weeks, the International Hotel has reported.

At $15 minimum a person that would mean he brought in more than $1.5 million in d i n n e r a n d cocktail show fees, not to mention gambling revenue.

A survey of 10 writers and hotel executives in Las Vegas indicated that P r e s l e y, who c l o s e d T h u r s d a y, has joined Frank Sinatra and Dean Martin as one of the city's top draws.

Martin drew more than 50,000 at the Riviera Hotel in a shorter period (three weeks) this summer, and was in a smaller show-room, capacity 1,200. The International holds 1,500 for dinner shows and 2,000 at midnight.

Sinatra made only 20 appearances in May at the 1,200-seat showroom at Caesars Palace. A capacity crowd saw most shows, and many were turned away from shows for all three performers.

The International, which opened July 2, said it had no figures on Barbra Streisand's opening four-week appearance. Despite poor opening n l g h t reviews, however, a trade publication reported she brought in about $900,000 for the huge show room.

Also mentioned as a top draw in the survey was Tom Jones, who appeared for four weeks in June at the 600-seat Flamingo Hotel showroom. It was the first year, however, the Welshman h a d d r a w n turnaway crowds.

"WE COVER THE NATION"

Thomas A. Parker
Exclusive Management

ELVIS PRESLEY

P.O.
417
MADISON,
TENN.

Dear Friend:

Elvis' first personal appearance in nine years at the
International Hotel in Las Vegas has been an exciting
show business event, heralded as such throughout the
nation's press and news reports and thoroughly enjoyed
by Elvis.  It gave him the opportunity to see fans of many
years who had come great distances and it was his great
hope that no one would be disappointed with his show.
The reaction of the record-breaking crowds was his answer -
Elvis had not disappointed them and they made that quite
evident by standing ovations every show of his month long
engagement.

A huge volume of congratulatory messages continues to pour
in and so Elvis wants you all to know how truly impressed
he is with your comments and sends you his most sincere
"thank you" for writing.

This appearance will serve as a springboard for many new
Elvis events and one of the first is the new single release
by RCA of a song introduced by Elvis during this personal
appearance, SUSPICIOUS MIND.  There is also the possibility
of an LP Album of this live performance but this will have
to await confirmation.

Presently, MGM has in release THE TROUBLE WITH GIRLS at
theatres and drive-in's everywhere and scheduled for fall
release is the NBC-Universal release CHANGE OF HABIT.

We will have a busy time catching up but we did want you
to know that your letter was appreciated.

Sincerely,


Col. Parker's Office

# up close with the king:
## one on one press interviews

A day or two after the opening show, two lucky British journalists were provided rare one on one access with Elvis.

**chris hutchins:** Elvis stayed to mingle with the press. He just wanted to please everybody that night. He was just so grateful that his first show had gone so well. Parker didn't like him mixing with people. He always told me that he protected the myth of Elvis. If people could talk to him and he got out there he would no longer be the unattainable Elvis. But I think he was also frightened of other people getting close to Elvis and influencing him and elbowing him out.

**RAY CONNOLLY** (music writer, *London Evening Standard*): A guy called Chris Hutchins organized my trip to Las Vegas to see Elvis, which I would review for the *London Evening Standard*. He was Tom Jones's PR and he knew the Colonel and told me he could get me to Elvis. For some reason I couldn't fly over to Las Vegas until the day of the show. I had an invitation and was on the plane flying from the UK to New York where I was to change flights and get one to Vegas. But the plane developed landing gear problems as it approached Kennedy airport and we had to circle for hours dumping all the fuel before they dare risk a landing which was miles away from the terminal and encircled by fire engines and ambulances. I thought, "This could be it, I'm not gonna see Elvis and I could die as well."

The plane eventually landed but it was terrifying moment and I missed the flight to Vegas and therefore missed the opening preview show, which was attended by all those celebrities like Cary Grant. I was at the show the next night and saw him an additional three times while in Vegas. Seeing him at the International was exciting but I was thinking, "Why's that orchestra behind him? He doesn't need it." But clearly that show was a triumph for Elvis. His music was fantastic and he had a great rhythm section. He did an awful lot of his early stuff and seemed to give the Sun stuff more respect than something like "All Shook Up" or "Don't Be Cruel," which he raced through. You could sense immediately his link with the audience. He felt at home. It worked tremendously well. It was as if everyone in the audience were his friends.

Chris Hutchins was a friend of the Colonel. Colonel always liked him. He got me and Don Short who wrote for *The Daily Mirror* into the show and to meet Elvis. Chris had always said, "You'll get to meet him" and after three days I was thinking it wasn't gonna happen. Suddenly the call came around 11PM, "Elvis will see you now." Me, Don Short, Chris Hutchins, and Terry O'Neill, who was a famous English photographer who later married Faye Dunaway and had a fling with Priscilla Presley, we all dashed upstairs. I had no time to bring a tape recorder, and went into a small sitting room in his suite. We were there for about 25 minutes. What was surprising was how nice he was. He was very thin and was wearing a black jumpsuit. He would answer any question you asked but the Colonel was standing in the back of this room and it was kind of intimidating.

It was bizarre. He was surrounded by his pals, no women in there. All these guys were sitting around and Elvis was drinking from a bottle of 7-Up. My big memory is asking him "Why did you do all those crummy films?" He just looked at me and told me he was in a rut and signed a contract and couldn't get out of it.

**elvis presley:** We've now completed all the deals I made when I came out of the army in 1960. And from now on, I'm going to play more serious parts and make fewer films. I wouldn't be being honest with you if I said I wasn't ashamed of some of the movies, and the songs I've had to sing in them. I would like to say they were good, but I can't. I've been extremely unhappy with that side of my career for some time. But how can you find 12 good songs for every film when you're making three films a year? I knew a lot of them were bad songs and they used to bother the heck out of me but I had to do them. They fitted the situation.

I get more pleasure out of performing to an audience like tonight, than any of the film songs have given me. How can you enjoy it when you have to sing songs to the guy you've just punched up? *(London Evening Standard/*August 2, 1969/Ray Connolly)

**ray connolly:** It was right to the point. That was Elvis's big problem, he threw away the '60s by doing those crummy movies. But appearing live was an up moment. He told me he was really excited about being back onstage.

**elvis presley:** We didn't decide to come back here for the money, I'll tell you that. I've always wanted to perform on the stage again for the last nine years, and it's been building inside of me since 1965 until the strain became intolerable. I got all het up about it, and I don't think I could have left it much longer. The time is just right. The money - I have no idea at all about that. I just don't want to know. You can stuff it. *(London Evening Standard/*August 2, 1969/Ray Connolly)

**ray connolly:** At that point, he looked back at the Colonel and there was a guffaw around the room. Then the Colonel said, "He can flush all his money away if he wants to, I won't care." And he did actually. (laughs) I'm looking at the very quick interview I wrote that night for the next edition of the morning's paper and he said, "Sometimes when I walk into a room at home and see all those gold records hanging around the walls I think they must belong to another person. Not me. I just can't believe it's me."

**don short:** Elvis was very quiet and reticent during the interview. He was very nice but was someone who was difficult to interview. He'd obviously taken advice from Parker. While he was very friendly, he was also extremely shy, almost as though he'd been briefed and maybe was deliberately holding back on prior instructions from Tom Parker and his PR advisors. He certainly wasn't giving too much away and didn't say anything sensational. Elvis was very different from his stage persona. I had great respect for him, I wasn't there to pick holes in him or push him hard. I didn't feel inhibited at all being around him.

The main target of my interview with Elvis was to talk about a European tour. I was trying to get a message back to European fans that he was gonna be traveling their way. He said he wanted to come to Europe and play London but there were no specific plans. We couldn't tie him down to make any commitments. We were hoping that he would make a commitment so we could please our readers and his fans in England who were longing to see him. He hadn't been in Europe since his military days.

**elvis presley:** I know I've been saying for years that I must visit Britain, and I will, I promise. But at the moment there are personal reasons why I can't. I shall be doing more shows in America now. I'm very satisfied with the reaction I've had here in Vegas. That's what the business is about for me. There will be films, too, but of a more serious nature, and I'll be making another television show for NBC. *(London Evening Standard/August 2, 1969/Ray Connolly)*

**RAY CONNOLLY:** At that time I was quite friendly with the Beatles. I was in Apple a few days before I left for Vegas and told Mal Evans, one of the Beatles' assistants, that I was going to Vegas to see Elvis. He was obsessed with Elvis, just like me. When we got to Elvis's room he had a telegram on his door from the Beatles and Mal. It said, "Congratulations on your opening night." Elvis seemed touched by that. He remembered meeting Mal and said, "Yeah, he's the guy in *Help* that kept swimming." Don (Short) asked him about the Beatles and he sang a little bit of "I Saw Her Standing There," (sings) "She was just seventeen, you know what I mean" and pretended to play guitar.

**ELVIS PRESLEY** (on the Beatles): I've recorded "Hey Jude". They're so interesting and so experimental. But I liked them particularly when they used to sing "she was just seventeen, you know what I mean" ("I Saw Her Standing There"). Did you see the telegram they sent me? *(London Evening Standard/August 2, 1969/Ray Connolly)*

**DON SHORT:** I talked to him about the Beatles. I don't think he saw them as a threat but he acknowledged their talent and thought they were a tremendous group and was complimentary about them.

**RAY CONNOLLY:** There was a lot of banter going on. I told him I liked the *Elvis is Back* album and wished he would do one more like that. He said, "I do too." The sad thing is he had all of these great plans and he didn't fulfill them because he got in another rut. He was gonna come to Europe. He was gonna make an R&B album.

**DON SHORT:** I wanted to know more about the man and the marriage. He didn't want to talk about his love life whatsoever. (laughs) That was rather funny when I asked him, "Can we have a little bit about Priscilla and the rumors that are flying around about your affairs with other women?" He just smiled at me and said, "I think that's best left unsaid." But he did it in a rather nice way and you accepted it.

**ELVIS PRESLEY:** When you're married you become aware of realities. Becoming a father made me realize a great deal more about life. *(London Evening Standard/August 2, 1969/Ray Connolly)*

**RAY CONNOLLY:** About two days after Elvis's Vegas shows, I was back in New York and went into Albert Grossman's office because I was trying to see (Bob) Dylan and he managed him. He said that he was in Woodstock. For some reason he suddenly put me on the phone with Dylan and I didn't know what to say to him because I hadn't planned to interview him. I told him I'd just been to see Elvis. From that moment instead of me being a Bob Dylan fan we were both Elvis fans. He asked me precisely, "What did he do? Did he do the Sun stuff? Did he do 'That's All Right, Mama'? Did he do 'Mystery Train'? Who's in the band?" Dylan read the *New York Times* review but he wanted to know what I thought of it. All these questions. Two days later I'm back in England and I'm on the phone with John Lennon and I get exactly the same questions from him about Elvis. "How was the show? Did he do any of the Sun numbers? Did he play 'Mystery Train'?" It showed me more than anything that rock stars are basically fans who do it themselves.

Questioned about the direction of his new songs, Elvis told *Newsweek*, "I go by the material. When I got 'In the Ghetto,' I couldn't turn it down. It was too big."

The magazine would go on to report, It's selling big, too, more than a million to date. Presley's plans include other personal appearances, through no dates have been specified, and more movie roles. "I'm going after more serious material," he said. "I'm tired of playing a guy who gets into a fight, then starts singing to the guy he's just beat up." And of course, the granddaddy of rock will continue trying to catch up with the times, sensing that he can't trade on the power of nostalgia forever. "There are a lot of new records out now that have the same sound I started. But they're better," he admitted, "I mean, you can't compare a song like 'Yesterday' with 'Hound Dog,' can you?" (*Newsweek*, August 11, 1969)

# viva Las vegas: the aftermath

**t.g. sheppard:** RCA's plan all along was to record a live album. Elvis had a lot of pressure on him for that first show so they didn't need to put more pressure on him and attempt to record opening night. They waited a few weeks for everybody to settle in and recorded some shows. The live album turned out great and sold very well.

**ronnie tutt:** He had such energy and power. Unfortunately, it never got transmitted to recording. They never captured that kind of energy that the man had. We couldn't wait until the show was over to go down and listen to the tracks. Later on, we were so discouraged because of the fact that the Colonel was responsible for messing up those tracks. They'd put Elvis's vocal like 70% of the sound, and the rhythm section way down. Elvis didn't know enough about producing to understand why his records really didn't have the power and energy that he felt. Because he stood right in front of me he could feel the power and energy from the drums all the time. (Elvis Australia/www.elvis.com/au/Arjan Deelen)

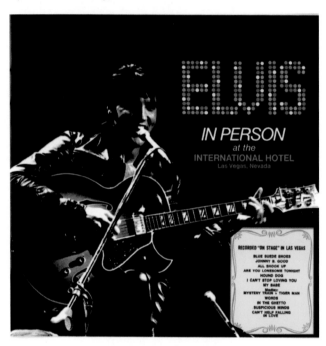

**james burton:** I was with him from '69 until he passed away. We didn't know we were making history, we were making music. We were living in the moment and doing something that we loved which was a blessing from God. I feel blessed to have spent all those years working with him.

**Lamar fike:** Vegas was a breaking ground to take his show on the road. And that's what it did. It proved to him and it proved to everybody else what he could do onstage. From then on out the road shows went like greased lightning. Elvis played Vegas eight weeks a year, which I thought was too damn much. But in between he could play other gigs. Vegas set up his whole money machine again.

**marty lacker:** Back then, Elvis was the only entertainer to come into Las Vegas who actually showed a profit in the showroom. He sold out both shows every night including the dinner show so they made money on the food, they made money on the tickets, and they made money on the drinks. They made sure the shows were not that long so they could get you back in the casino. At that time, it was the gambling that counted. They'd give away food, they'd give away drinks, they'd give away rooms and they'd give away tickets to shows. And you didn't have to be a high roller to get those things. They wanted you to stay in the hotel, go to the gambling tables and lose your damn money. Their philosophy was if we make you happy you're gonna stay and the longer they stayed the more money they lost.

Before Elvis came to Las Vegas, the normal schedule for an entertainer was they'd work six days and were off on Monday. Elvis was enjoying performing so much, especially in the beginning, that he wanted to perform seven nights a week. Nobody had done that before.

That forced other performers to follow his lead because the hotels would say, "Elvis Presley works seven days a week, why can't you?"

**MYRNA SMITH:** Out of all the years that we worked with Elvis it seemed that his energy level was highest during that first engagement. Through the years I've worked with Aretha Franklin, Tom Jones and Wilson Pickett but it was Elvis who gave out the most energy to an audience and the audience responded right back with their own energy.

**GORDON STOKER:** Having performed with Elvis in the '50s and '60s and seeing him live in Vegas in the '70s he hadn't changed. He was no different, it's just the show was more dressy and he was still a ball of energy and still had that beautiful smile. He was a perfectionist. He wanted to sing everything just right and he did.

**bobby vinton:** What I'll always remember about Elvis is him saying, "I kind of envy you" and I said, "I don't understand, what do you mean?" And he said, "You're so relaxed, you get out on stage and sing and play all of the instruments. In my case people expect so much from me. When I go on stage I've gotta be the King and it puts a lot of pressure on me. It's hard to live up to those expectations every night. What makes it so rough is I haven't performed live in many years. I don't have the confidence like you do 'cause you do it every night." I remember telling him, "Elvis, I've gotta play all the instruments and stand on my head, you don't have to do that stuff." He said, "No no, I've got to be the greatest thing you ever saw!" He had to be better than people remembered and that put a lot of pressure on him. In a way I kind of felt a little sad for him. "God Elvis, you don't need to worry about all of that stuff, just show up."

**jimmy newman:** Elvis was the top draw in Vegas, more so than other top stars like Frank Sinatra, Dean Martin and Tom Jones.

**petula clark:** Before Elvis, Vegas was Sinatra and The Rat Pack. Elvis changed the image of Vegas when he came back in '69. It was a different atmosphere altogether seeing Elvis.

**george klein:** Elvis came out and rocked that city like it had never been rocked before. He reinvented Vegas and did it in his style.

**mike weatherford** (author, *Cult Vegas*): Timing is everything in show business. The International came along as the first example of Vegas thinking really big, on this huge scale as far as the 3,000 plus hotel rooms, which have become the standard now. So they opened this big hotel and it didn't have an identity until Elvis came along so whenever he came to town he filled up the place and it became all about him. Vegas needed some help by then. It was certainly losing its luster. Now the Rat Pack had been completely glamorized and completely reinvented. But back then the Rat Pack weren't cool anymore. By the late '60s, early '70s they had aged to the point where during the counterculture movement they were doing the bad TV specials, reading the cue cards and carrying the "We want broads!" sign. (laughs) Vegas was lapsing into the Bill Murray parody era.

I also think Elvis sort of ushered in the low rollers era. Back in the '50s you can look at the aerial maps of the Stardust and you can see these symmetrical barracks of motel units. So already in the '50s they were getting away from the glamorous Sands Hotel high rollers, the guys with the pinkie rings betting tons of money. (laughs) Joe Delaney, a veteran writer from the *Las Vegas Sun,* analyzed when Elvis and Sinatra were in town at the same time. The gist of what he said was Elvis did the volume business and Sinatra did the quality business. Sinatra played showrooms at Caesar's for 800 to 1400 people. With Elvis they were ignoring fire codes and packing the balcony (laughs) and filling it up with all these fans that came in just to see him. Without Elvis you wondered what the International would have done. As it was, Elvis gave that hotel an identity coming in two times a year.

The timing was also good as far as Elvis's fans. The original '50s fans had become old enough to be casino customers. They were there anyway and he was reaching out to the people that had grown up with him. Las Vegas has always kind of been geared to the demographic of 45-year-old plus with the discretionary income. So Elvis coming to Vegas in '69 hit that perfectly on the head.

**dave clark:** When the DC5 played Vegas we didn't play in the casinos, we played in the big sports arena. As a rock and roll performer, Elvis made it work playing in a casino in Vegas. Frank Sinatra was the only other performer who really did that successfully but he and the Rat Pack were from another era. The experience of playing Vegas wasn't like going to screaming concerts like the DC5 had or the Beatles or Elvis had when he was playing arenas in the '50s. Vegas was a different ballgame and Elvis took a risk playing there because he was going for a different type of audience, a cross-section. Elvis brought the young people into Vegas, which was exciting, as well as the regular Vegas crowd.

**t.g. sheppard:** Elvis brought people in from every country around the world. During his shows in Vegas I'd look out into the audience and see every nationality in the world, people from France and Japan and Denmark and England. It was international at the International Hotel. (laughs)

**patti parry:** Elvis made Las Vegas. Nobody ever filled a showroom like Elvis did, and he did it over and over and over again.

**t.g. sheppard:** What he also brought to Vegas was a huge revenue stream. His shows made tons of money for the hotel and the city.

**lamar fike:** Elvis was the biggest money maker in Vegas. Elvis did it by volume; Sinatra did it by high rollers. But Elvis beat everybody into the ground by the sheer volume of people he brought in. So by volume they spent more money than any of the high rollers ever did. When Elvis died the lights went dim in Vegas. They dimmed the lights on purpose.

**myram borders:** The Las Vegas Convention and Visitor's Authority promotes Las Vegas around the world. For many of their international trips and events, the media and travel agency executives will have a showgirl and an Elvis impersonator with them. Las Vegas has very few showgirls anymore and it certainly doesn't have an Elvis.

**mike weatherford:** Today, Las Vegas is primarily associated with two images, the showgirl and Elvis and both have taken on a life of their own. Anything they do around the country to promote Las Vegas it's Elvis in a sequined jumpsuit and a show girl. The show girl was originally imported from the Lido & the Follies in Paris, and it was a real French image and Las Vegas totally stole that and appropriated it. In the same way they've appropriated Elvis's image in the sequined jumpsuit as kind of a branding.

**sonny west:** When you think of Elvis now you think of Vegas. When you think of Vegas you think of Elvis. That city came alive when he was in town. For those two months a year he played Vegas, he made that city jump and you could just feel the excitement that he created. Elvis is the all-time king of Vegas. He set attendance records that no one is ever gonna break.

# king of the whole wide world

**lisa marie presley:** Seeing him in Vegas was an amazing and incredible experience to watch. I was constantly in awe.

**NANCY SINATRA:** It was my first time in a big nightclub and I was scared to death so I went up to rehearse during the day and Elvis was performing at night. Barbra (Streisand) opened the hotel, then Elvis followed her and I followed him. I was way out of my league but the entertainment director wanted me. My dad and I went to Elvis's closing show. He was phenomenal and he got better and better. Oh God, Elvis was brilliant! It was quite a wonderful experience. Elvis's audiences were absolutely crazy. They just adored him and he knew it and he gave back that

love to them. Elvis and Priscilla came to see my opening show, which was just lovely. My dad sent out invitations to all his movie star friends so we had Kirk Douglas, Yul Brunner and Jack Benny, all kinds of people. It was a huge showroom. For me the International Hotel was an intimidating place to play because I didn't have enough fans to fill that kind of a room. They were able to drape it off for me so it didn't look so empty.

In my show, I wore a two-piece white outfit with glitter and fringe on it. It's funny, the next year I went to see Elvis and he was in all white, fringe and glitter. (laughs) I was like, "Oh God, the little stinker!" (laughs) Elvis was wearing my outfit.

**SONNY WEST:** Elvis's shows in Vegas were dynamite in '69, '70, '71 up through the early part of '72. Then after that he kind of got into a groove doing the show and we were on the road. It was tiring to keep going like that. But he loved to work and wanted to work as much as possible. For those two or three years he looked fantastic and felt great. Then of course it all culminated with the '73 satellite show in Hawaii and he looked like a Greek god. Jerry Weintraub, the promoter and now film producer, told Elvis that he couldn't pull off the satellite show but Colonel pulled it off and got over 40 countries that bought satellite time. No one's done it since then.

**joe moscheo:** We had an hour and a half break between the dinner show and the midnight show and I remember for that first night a lot of people came downstairs to see him. They were waiting in the hallway outside of his dressing room, which was the first dressing room when you got off the elevator. It was a big suite. We went out in the hallway to mingle and noticed everyone just waiting to see Elvis. Huge movie stars. People like Cary Grant, Sammy Davis Jr. He finally came out and greeted everyone. They were all Elvis fans. They'd never seen anything like it. Sammy Davis Jr. was one of the most talented guys in the world but he was in awe of Elvis. Elvis had something that none of them had. He had that strong connection with the people and the charisma to match it, as witnessed over 30 years since his death. Today he's more popular now than he was when he was alive.

**MARTY LACKER:** George Klein and I saw Elvis's show on the second night of the first engagement.

**GEORGE KLEIN:** Elvis wanted to blow everybody away. But he wasn't sure how he'd be accepted. We were all there to back him and show our support and make him feel comfortable. But he really didn't need us, man. (laughs) He was on from the word *go*.

**MARTY LACKER:** We sat in Elvis's booth and after the show Joe (Esposito) came to get us and brought us backstage. Elvis was so anxious to hear what we had to say that he was outside of the dressing room door waiting for me and George. He had a big smile on his face and we hugged. I told him how much we loved the show.

**GEORGE KLEIN:** You could see the happiness in his face and how overwhelmed he was. He knew he came back and conquered the audience. He was back in his element that he loved so much. It was the first time I'd seen him that happy in a long, long time.

**bill medley:** I saw him during his first engagement back in Vegas in '69 and it was magic. He was one of the great singers with such a great voice but he was Elvis Presley. When I saw him the audience was just going crazy. I'm not sure other than to sing his songs and sing them great that there was a real opportunity for Elvis to perform a lot because of all the screaming and the girls wanting to kiss him. It's kind of like the Beatles. One of the reasons the Beatles stopped touring is people wouldn't listen to them.

**gordon stoker:** In Vegas he told me, "At first I didn't understand why the Jordanaires and Scotty (Moore) and D.J. (Fontana) quit me because I didn't get the full story from the Colonel." The Colonel was always good at not telling the complete story. I wish the Colonel or Tom Diskin had told him the real story. He said, "Had I known you had that much work, I wouldn't have wanted to stand in your way." He also said, "If I had something like that to hold me in Memphis I certainly would have stayed." I'll always appreciate that he told me that.

**andy klein** (concert attendee): At age 17, I flew to Las Vegas by myself to see Elvis for two nights in the middle of his first week of shows in August 1969. For one show, a $20 tip to the maître d' gave me a seat at the far left table of the first row. I managed to shake Elvis's hand. I then jokingly yelled, "Elvis, sing 'Queenie Wahine's Papaya'". This song from the movie *Paradise, Hawaiian Style* was arguably not only the worst song ever recorded by Elvis, it was probably the worst song ever recorded by a human being. Elvis heard me and laughed. And so ended my first and only "conversation" with Elvis. A guy nearby heard me and looked at me as if I was crazy to request such a ridiculous song. He obviously didn't get the joke. But to me, it was more than just a joke. It was my way of communicating to Elvis that he had come such a long way from the abysmal movie years. The Elvis standing on stage in Las Vegas was light years away from the Elvis appearing on screen in *Paradise, Hawaiian Style*. In just a few short years, Elvis had transformed himself from a disappointing movie star with unfilled potential to the greatest live performer the world had ever seen.

**jerry schilling:** Back in the '70s, Elvis and Priscilla and me and my wife, Sandy went to see Sammy Davis Jr. After the show we went backstage and hung out with Sammy and his wife, Altovise. Sammy and Elvis were magic together. Sammy had that great personality and he kept Elvis laughing. It was after the late show and Elvis said, "Would you guys like to come over to our hotel up to the suite?" We all go in the car and go back to the Hilton and as we're walking through the lobby going to the elevators we heard a very familiar Chuck Berry intro. And Sammy and Elvis just looked at each other and with a smile we all just turned around without

anything being said and we headed for the lounge. There was one table of people, maybe two. The whole lounge was about empty. We went down to a booth in front and Elvis was a fun guy. He would holler out a tune. Chuck saw that it was Elvis and said, "Hey Elvis, remember when we were battling for number one and you had this song and I had the other song?" The real payoff was when Elvis said, "Do 'Promised Land'!" And he's sitting with Sammy Davis Jr. and they're singing the lines along with Chuck about a poor boy wanting to go clean through Mississippi.

**sonny west:** I remember seeing Ringo in Vegas. Red and I asked him if he remembered playing pool with us and he said, "Yes, I do." He said, "I won, didn't I" (laughs). So Elvis got to meet up with him again. When the Beatles first came to America and did that press conference at the airport and someone said they'd heard that Elvis was a big influence on them when they were younger. Ringo stepped up and said, "I don't know what you mean!" and started acting like Elvis, moving and jiggling. Elvis saw that and he got a big kick out of it.

**ringo starr** (The Beatles): The second time I met Elvis, they took me to Vegas because of the video for my song "Sentimental Journey," the one where I was dressed up with the bow tie and the dancing girls (laughs). They said, "Oh, he can play Vegas now." (laughs) It was just far out.

**RINGO STARR:** Elvis was great. Really fantastic. He was everything he's cracked up to be, and more. (*Disc and Music Echo*/February 7, 1970)

> **RINGO STARR:** Elvis's show was good but it was a bit scary for me. It was fine seeing Elvis but the idea of me playing that huge room was pretty scary. Anyway they decided to fly me in so I could have a look at it. I thought, I might as well see a good show. There's a great thing in the *Beatles Anthology* DVD, and we're talking about meeting Elvis. It's confusing to all of us. George (Harrison) said he met him a couple of times (Madison Square Garden 1972) and he does his story. For me, I felt I just kept bumping into Elvis. (laughs)

**bobby vinton:** I either opened the day before him or the day after at the Flamingo Hotel. In my dressing room was a six-foot high guitar made out of red roses because of my song, "Roses Are Red" and there was a little note attached that said, "Good luck on your opening tonight, Elvis." I'd never received anything like that from any other entertainer in Vegas before or since. That shows you how classy he was. Early on in his engagement we bumped into each other in one of the lounges. He told me he had "Roses Are Red" on his jukebox.

> **dave clark:** I spent a couple of hours offstage with Elvis in Vegas in '69 and I found him to be very real. He was very down to earth and it was lovely to see somebody who'd had that amazing success was still a real person. He could also make fun of himself, which really impressed me. I remember him saying to me, "If you've seen one of my movies Dave, you've seen them all. It's just a different location and different songs." (laughs)

**paul anka:** I saw Elvis perform "My Way" in Vegas. It was huge because I knew he was going through this turmoil in his life. You felt his struggle and you felt the pain he was going through. It was also huge because he was huge--the magnification of the artist and their life and their persona and all of their charisma comes to play when you hit a song like that. It's not like going into a lounge and hearing a lounge singer do "My Way." When I heard Elvis do "My Way" with the big orchestra at the Hilton it carried a lot of emotion. Elvis was a great stylist and he made it his own, which I think is the key to any great artist. "My Way" became this incredible badge on this guy because he was fighting some demons. He was a very very important artist in the culture of pop music.

> **pat boone:** I saw several of his openings through the years in Las Vegas. Once I went back-stage to visit with him in the dressing room and he said, "Hey, let's go back here in this closet." It was a great big walk in closet. He wanted to get away so we could talk. He said, "I gotta show you something, man. " He brought out this badge that President Nixon had given him that made him a narcotics agent. I thought, this is sort of preposterous. He's not out there amongst drug dealers. How's he gonna put the finger on anybody? (laughs) But he was so proud of it.

**jerry schilling:** Out of all the celebrities that Elvis met through the years, I think he was most excited to meet Jack Lord. Elvis would spend time with a lot of celebrities. We'd finish the first show in Vegas and Elvis would say, "Would you take Mr. and Mrs. Lord up to the suite, I'm gonna have dinner with them." He always spoke softly because they were real classy people. He really had a reverence around Jack Lord. It was amazing. The only other people that I saw Elvis have that kind of respect for were his in-laws, Priscilla's mother and father.

**bill medley:** I was performing solo in the lounge at the International while Elvis was playing in the showroom. Elvis would go on at eight o' clock, I'd go on at ten, he'd go on at midnight and I'd go on at two in the morning. At that time Elvis was singing "You've Lost That Lovin' Feeling" in the main room. So after his eight o 'clock show Elvis and his boys were walking through the back and headed up to his room. They heard me onstage and I was doing "Lovin' Feeling". Elvis said, "Let's go in and see Bill." And somebody said, "Well, he's on stage." Elvis said, "Well, let's go walk onstage and say hi." So I'm onstage and I'm doing "Lovin' Feeling" and I look to my left and I see somebody walking at me, which onstage is enough to scare the shit out of you. I looked again and it was Elvis and that was even more remarkable. Elvis and I were good friends so it wasn't a total freak-out. So he walks by me and I was in the section of the song, (sings) "Baby, baby, I get down on my knees for you..." and he walked by, hit me on the arm and said, (imitates Elvis), "Hi Bill." (laughs) and then he was gone. The audience freaked, I damn near didn't get them back.

Vegas was still small enough that the whole town knew that Elvis Presley had been onstage with Bill Medley at his ten o'clock show. So that for my next show at two AM, there were lines waiting to get in. I was doing good business but I didn't usually have big lines to get in to see me at two o'clock in the morning. They were there thinking maybe Elvis will show up. And sure enough, I'm in the same place in the song and here here comes again. But this time it's him and about ten of his Memphis Mafia guys and about ten security guards. And they all walked by me, hit me on the arm and said, "Hi Bill." (laughs) I finished the song and people were freaking out. They finally calmed down and I said, "Okay, I don't know who he is but now he's starting to piss me off." (laughs)

**john wilkinson:** The only thing that wasn't planned were the monologues in between songs. Some took 10 to 15 minutes. Colonel Parker wasn't too happy about them, and he soon told Elvis to 'stop talking'. "Elvis wasn't too impressed, and he said 'look – these people know that I can sing, and they want to know more about me. They need to know where I come from. There's a lot of people out there that had a much harder time than I did when I was growing up and if they're spending a lot of money to see my show, they have the right to know where I come from and what I feel and by the way – if you take care of the business, I'll take care of the show.' And he walked off. That was Elvis. We had enough songs to play non stop for 48 hours if we wanted to, but he wanted people to see that he wasn't an artist that just got lucky."
(*Memories: On the Road with Elvis and John Wilkinson*/Peter Verbruggen)

**june juanico** (former girlfriend): In August of 1969, Hurricane Camille devastated my hometown of Biloxi, Mississippi and we had no running water or electricity. My husband, the one that I married on the rebound from Elvis, took me out to Las Vegas. I saw one of Elvis's shows in mid to late August. My brother-in-law, Wally kept telling me that he and Elvis were buddies. I didn't believe him and thought he was full of bull. So we're out there and Wally told me he had connections at the International and could get us tickets to see Elvis. So he made arrangements for us to go to the first show. I hadn't seen Elvis since '63. Elvis didn't know I was coming out to the Vegas show. I was sitting with my elbow resting on the stage. My brother-in-law kept yelling at me, "June, stand up so he can see you!" So finally when I decided to stand up, Elvis started walking in my direction. We sort of made eye contact. He put his hand up to block out the lights and I think he saw me. Every few songs he'd glance over my way and block his eyes from the lights. Like I said, I think he thought it was me but he wasn't sure.

When I went on tour with him in Florida in '56 Elvis was on a natural high whenever he was onstage and he was the same way in Vegas. He was just magnificent. Maybe it's just a love that never dies but my heart pounded throughout the entire show. I was probably still in love with him. I think he was the love of my life. He was very thin and his left leg was shaking so fast, it was in triple time to the beat of his music. That's when he first started putting karate moves into his act. I'd never really seen him that dynamic and polished. His voice was out of this world. He just lit up the entire stage. He was in control of every note he played. Elvis was always in charge of his music. His sound was his and he did it like he wanted to do with it. He moved with every beat and he covered the entire stage. He made eye contact with everybody there. He was a lot more polished and a lot more in control than he was when I saw him perform in the '50s. This time instead of just a three piece-band, he had an orchestra, backup singers and the sound was better because of the technology. Back then they were saying he sounded like he was singing through a tin can on a stick.

Later on that night, my brother-in-law called Joe Esposito and he put me on the phone with Elvis. I talked to him for about fifteen, twenty minutes and he said, "I knew it was you!" He said, "I haven't been able to get you off of my mind. Did you make out okay with the hurricane?" It has been about ten days since the storm hit and it had been worldwide news. It was the worst disaster to hit the U.S. until Hurricane Katrina. Then he asked me about every friend, ever house he stayed in, every hangout, every building, every lounge from when we spent time together back in the '50s. He remembered everything. We had a wonderful conversation. The conversation ended when he said, "Baby, I can't believe how bad your timing is? " I said, "About what?" He said, "I would really love to spend some time with you while you're here but Priscilla came in this morning." We used to call one another by our first and last names. I said, "Well, let me let you go, take this thought with you, I love you Elvis Presley and I always will." He said, "I love you too June Juanico and I always will."

**JEAN-MARC GARGIULO** (concert attendee): My friends and I came from Paris to see Elvis and we saw him live on August 12th. That morning, I called Colonel Parker, who I'd corresponded with for years while running the "Treat Me Nice" fan club in France. He sent his assistant, Tom Diskin down to meet us in the coffee shop. We had a nice conversation and at the end of the talk we said matter of factly, "When are we going to met Elvis?" And he said, "I'll see what I can do." He took our number. We were staying at a cheap place called the Holiday Motel because it was too expensive to stay at the International. My three friends, Marius, Marie-Chantal and Mathieu and I arrived at the hotel for the dinner show. Colonel Parker recognized us inside the showroom--I'm not sure how--and said, "Are you the Frenchie?" So we said "Yes." He asked,

Elvis with fan Jean-Marc Gargiulo

"Where's your table?' and we had a table in the back of the showroom. He asked, "Did you get my message?" and we said, "No Sir." He said, "After the show, don't move, I'll come get you." We knew right then that we were going to meet Elvis. When the show was done he brought us backstage. Some American fans were following us and he told the security guard, "Just the French." We went through the kitchen and stood outside Elvis's dressing room door. First, the Colonel brought in a blind kid. When the door opened to let the kid inside I saw Elvis, and went "Oh my God it's him!" Maybe five minutes later the door opens and Colonel said, "Come in French." Elvis was sitting on a big chair and he stood up to greet us. Colonel Parker introduced us as the French fan club. Elvis said, "Bonsoir, bonsoir, bonsoir" and he repeated it about 12 times. "He said, "I'm sorry but that's the only French I can remember." (laughs) The first thing he said was "Have you seen the show?" And we told him "yes." He asked, "Did you like it?" He asked if he was still popular in France and we told him "of course." He was amazed we came so far to see him. I also remember him asking if we had enough money. We told him we were fine. When we met with Tom Diskin, I gave him a poster I had made up of a big Elvis meeting in July that I'd organized in Versailles (France) that over 1500 Elvis fans attended from eight different countries. Colonel pulled out the poster and said, "Look what they brought you." Elvis took the poster in his hand and took a long look at it and said, "This is nice, can I keep it?," which made us feel good. Then my friends and I started talking to each other in French and Elvis asked, "Hmm...what you say?" We told him we were talking about how we were fans of the way he moved in the '50s in films like *Jailhouse Rock,* particularly on the song "You're So Square (Baby I Don't Care)". One of my friends imitated one of his leg movements and Elvis laughed. We asked if he would be doing any of those movements onstage and he said, "I'll see what I can do." And during the midnight show he did it during "All Shook Up." We also asked him when he was coming to Europe and he said, "In the next six months." Then he signed some autographs and took photos with us. What was amazing was he was making most of the conversation with us. He made us feel like he was a friend. He was down to earth and didn't act like a star.

**RODNEY BINGENHEIMER:** I went to the closing night of Elvis's '69 engagement with a girl named Terry. That night he wore a white jumpsuit unlike the black one he wore at the opening show. He sang "Runaway" that night and Del Shannon was in the audience. Terry and I went to the party afterwards in this banquet room and I spoke to him there and took a photo of him drinking a Bloody Mary. I gave Elvis a copy of GO magazine and he asked for a subscription to the magazine. A bunch of celebrities were there—Nancy Sinatra, Jimmy Webb, Bill Medley, Johnny Rivers, and Trini Lopez. The next night was the big opening for Nancy Sinatra and I went to that too. Elvis and Priscilla were there. There was a party in a suite after the show. People like Frank and Tina Sinatra, Kirk Douglas, Tom Jones, Natalie Wood, Burt Lancaster, Anthony Newley, Mitzi Gaynor, Hugh O'Brien, and Jack Jones showed up. We all got to rap to Elvis. Elvis introduced me to Frank Sinatra at that party.

**T.G. SHEPPARD:** I wish people could have seen the real show and that was the show each night after the show upstairs on the 30th floor in his suite. Everybody would gather around the piano and sing gospel songs until daylight. The private shows were always the most electrifying. Each time I was ever in his presence, which was for a lot of years, I drank in every moment that I had with him, whether it was backstage or on the Lisa Marie or one on one watching Monty Python on TV. I knew then as I do now that I was in the presence of greatness.

**MYRNA SMITH:** Elvis was a kid at heart. He played lots of pranks on us. He'd use water guns. That was his way of letting off some steam and having fun.

**ESTELLE BROWN:** It was around Halloween time. For some reason he wanted me to shake his hand, which I did and when he pulled his arm back, a hand was still in my hand. And I thought I would pass out. It was a rubber hand. (laughs) That's the kind of joke he would play on us. He'd do all sorts of crazy things. I remember he came out with a monkey mask onstage. He'd lie on the floor and sing Christmas carols.

**JIMMY MULIDORE** (alto sax, clarinet, flute, oboe and piccolo, Joe Guercio Orchestra): During the quiet part of "American Trilogy," I played the flute solo. Elvis said he wanted it to have the feel of someone sitting under a tree in Georgia in the middle of a sweltering summer representing Dixie. It was very dramatic; it went from thundering music and vocal to this very quiet section. It was a defining moment of that song and it would give Elvis a short rest while the spotlight was put on me. It was a very difficult solo and you really had to concentrate to get it right. Elvis was a prankster. Every night Elvis and some of the guys from the Memphis Mafia, Red West and Sonny West would take squirt guns and squirt water between my face and the flute so I'd slip and mess up the solo. Elvis was proud to see that I never missed a note.

**Nicholas Naff:** Elvis's dressing room was private but a door in his dressing room opened into a reception area. We'd carefully select who was allowed to go down there to greet the artist. The greeting area was always a bustle of activity. I'd spend time in his dressing room almost every night. Elvis exuded a certain shyness. He spoke softly and was very polite. He had a certain soft charm to him and a quick wit.

**Gordon Stoker:** My wife and I caught Elvis's show in Vegas quite often. He'd always mention that I was in the audience. He was very appreciative and always invited us up to his room after the show. He was just a wonderful guy to be around. He'd take a shower, put on different clothes and then come out and talk with us. He was just a genuine person, just a lot of fun to be around. He'd always say to my wife, Jean and I, "You've got to come back to my second show, that first show wasn't any good." I said, "Elvis, that show was wonderful." And he'd say, "Oh no, I can do better." That's what I think killed him. He always wanted to do the second show better than the first.

**Loanne Miller Parker:** The other casinos loved it when Elvis came to town. They had their own high rollers who'd want to go to Elvis's show. At that time the hotels would exchange reservations with one another. If I worked at Caesar's Palace and I had a high roller who wanted to see the Elvis show, I'd call someone in the casino at the International Hotel and say, "I need a reservation for a party of eight" and they would honor that. Maybe the next month Frank Sinatra would be at Caesar's and the International would call them for a reservation they'd need for a high roller. The casino people were happy to get any VIP high rollers from other casinos because you could not reach the showroom without going through the casino. Quite often on the way out from Elvis's show they would stop in the casino and do a little gambling.

**Patti Parry:** He was like a prisoner in his hotel room. It's a tough life. He was a prisoner of his own fame. He couldn't go anywhere 'cause you couldn't miss Elvis Presley! (laughs). When he went down to the casino they would knock over tables trying to get to him. Sometimes we'd sneak out to see the Clara Ward Singers at the New Frontier Hotel or we'd see Jimmy Dean. To prevent Elvis from being recognized, we'd go in after the room was dark and leave before the show ended. We were like vampires. We were nocturnal. We stayed up all night and slept all day.

**Sonny West:** When he was in Vegas he didn't go out much. He was unavailable. He was invisible. You didn't see him 'til he hit that stage and he was wound up and ready to go, unless you were one of those fans who found a way to sneak back in those corridors to meet him.

**Lisa Marie Presley:** I love "How Great Thou Art". I was around and watched him record it and went to all the shows in the '70s. There's a song called "It's Over" that killed me. There's a song called "Mary in the Morning" that I just love. There's some obscure ones that were never singles. "Separate Ways" wasn't paid nearly enough attention as it should have been. It's really beautiful. I love "Just Pretend," that killed me. I also love "You Gave Me a Mountain" too.

**Millie Kirkham:** I'd worked with Elvis since 1957. I sang backgrounds on songs like "Blue Christmas," "Don't," "Devil in Disguise," "Surrender," "Just Pretend" and "The Wonder of You". I was working in Nashville doing sessions every day and Elvis asked me to come out to Vegas because they were filming for *That's The Way It Is*. Ordinarily I wouldn't have since they were filming for that I did it. They filmed five or six of our stage shows. Most of the songs in the show were things I'd recorded with him.

**jimmy mulidore:** I'd visit Elvis in his suite after many of the shows. Elvis would sit at the bar and greet everyone. He was the nicest southern gentleman you'd ever meet. It was always really festive. There were a million beautiful women up there every night and a great spread of food and drink. He'd play the piano and sing and everyone would gather around and join in.

**loanne miller parker:** A lot of people say it wasn't fair for Elvis to work that hard but what they forget is all the acts worked that hard. When it reached the point where they were touring and doing the Las Vegas engagements Colonel saw that this wasn't beneficial for Elvis. A few years in, he renegotiated with the hotel that Elvis would now only do one show a night and two on weekends.

**t.g. sheppard:** He brought an excitement to the strip that I've never seen before. There was just something very magical about him. His karma and his charisma was so powerful that you couldn't help but stare and that first night back in Vegas when he walked out onstage, those in the audience couldn't help but stare because they were watching history. The word icon is not big enough. They were watching a force onstage of energy that was so strong. Elvis was the kind of person that if you were in a room and your back was to the door you felt his presence instantly without seeing him come into the room.

**bill medley:** I'd be getting ready for my show and so would Elvis. He'd call me and say "Come on over to the dressing room." I'd go over about ten minutes before the show was about to start, everybody would leave his dressing room and it would just be me and Elvis and his hairdresser. We talked as guys, Elvis and Bill. We had a good friendship. He knew he could trust me. He knew I was an artist who cared about the guy Elvis, not Elvis Presley. I made that very clear to him and his people. I must say one of the most interesting experiences in my life was one time we were talking right before he was gonna go on. He said, "Bill, why don't you come up, I'm going on." So I went up and we're talking on the way. He's kind of in the shadows. They're dealing with his clothes and someone's messing with his hair. Then the lights went out and the girls start screaming. I kind of backed up and chills came over me. For the first time I realized, "Holy shit, that's Elvis Presley!"

**frank lieberman:** James Bacon was a well known columnist for the *Hollywood Reporter* and he was also a friend of Howard Hughes. He became the main columnist for the Herald-Examiner. Jim and I were up in Vegas and we went backstage after Elvis's show. He knew Colonel Parker and had met Elvis on the movie sets. We knew Sammy Shore and were in his dressing room. Out in the hallway was Colonel Parker. I was very naïve, I didn't know anything. I introduced myself to Colonel Parker and said, "I'd like to do an interview with Elvis." And he literally laughed in my face. He said, "Young man, Elvis doesn't do interviews and if he would do an interview, he certainly wouldn't do it with a local paper. If he did an interview it would be with a big newspaper and they'd have to pay me to do it." I said, "Sir, I'm not trying to be rude but I will do an interview with Elvis Presley." I didn't get to meet Elvis that night but the following Wednesday my rave review of Elvis's opening night show ran in the newspaper. (*Los Angeles Herald-Examiner*, "Elvis IS still the King!" February 4, 1970). The next weekend I went back to Vegas and saw the show again. When the show was over the maître d' said I had to go to the house phone and call this gentleman named Joe Esposito. Joe told me to go backstage

and a security guard would escort me to Elvis Presley's dressing room. I thought, "Holy shit, what did I do?" I walked into the dressing room and on the back wall behind the sofa was a blow-up of my review. Elvis came out, introduced himself and thanked me for this "wonderful review." He said, "What can I do for you?" I said, "Well, the Colonel said I can't do it but I'd like to do an interview with you." So he said, "Okay, let's go in the room right here and we'll do an interview." I said, "I don't have my tape recorder" and he said, "Don't worry about it, just write your notes down." I'm taking notes as quick as I can and my hands are shaking. Elvis was delightful. I didn't know what to ask because it was spur of the moment but it worked out okay. I finished the interview, ran up to my room and made sure I could read all my notes and wrote my story. It ran the following weekend in the newspaper. I was young and naïve and had no idea of what I had. I'd interviewed Barbra Streisand a few weeks earlier but I was prepared. Elvis Presley was different, he was the person. I started getting phone calls from fellow journalists and wire services wanting to know if there was more to the story than I had in the paper. Then I found out no one had done a real sit-down interview with him in many years. That was the beginning of our friendship. That interview led to me writing stories for the old movie magazines like *Photoplay*. He would give me a little bit of information, personal stuff like who he was seeing or what was happening in his life, and then it was up to me to exaggerate about it in the magazines. He'd try to figure out which stories I wrote in those movie magazines because I never used my real name. He got a kick out of it. But he also would get pissed at me because I wrote bad reviews of his shows too. If I saw a show that wasn't good I'd write about it honestly. In one of them I wrote that he looked glassy eyed and he didn't like that at all. "What do you mean I look glassy-eyed? What are you talking about?!"

**rodney bingenheimer:** After Elvis's first engagement in Las Vegas ended the next month I went to Toronto for the Rock and Roll Revival Show. It had the Doors, Alice Cooper, Little Richard, Jerry Lee Lewis, and Gene Vincent. And of course John Lennon and Yoko came to the show and played. The guy who arranged the festival, John Brower, and I went to the airport in a Cadillac limousine and picked up John and Yoko. In the car, I told John that I taped Elvis's opening show in Vegas. I played him the tape of Elvis singing "Yesterday" and "Hey Jude" from that first show and he was excited. He said, "Very cool, man, very cool." He got a big kick out of it.

**rona barrett:** There are certain events that are so momentous and make such a change in one's life. When Elvis arrived back in Las Vegas he was somebody you could not forget. He helped make Las Vegas the glittering capital of entertainment.

# elvis for everyone

**phil everly** (The Everly Brothers): There is no other "king" but Elvis.

**pete townshend** (The Who): Elvis was the first truly beautiful man, rather than a rugged handsome man, that young men like me, and Roger (Daltrey), felt safe to adore. Maybe it was because his early music was so blues based. His legacy is muddled. We have to focus on early work, and just one or two of his movies, and elements of his TV shows, to keep his memory pure. People now know that Elvis could play a mean rhythm guitar himself, and needed no other musicians to perform a great song. But Elvis was not just a rock star, he was an all-round entertainer. He flew on our adoration for the last ten years of his life and he is probably still flying on it now.

**roger daltrey** (The Who): Elvis changed my life. He looked like he came from Mars. It was like he was from outer space. When people saw him, they were like, "What the hell is that making that noise?" He was just so inspiring. In England, Elvis opened the door to us hearing people like Little Richard, Jackie Wilson, James Brown and all the Chicago blues guys.

**paul simon:** The first thing I remember about Elvis was sitting in the back seat of my parents' car and hearing a disc jockey say, "Whenever this guy sings in the south, girls scream and jump around and his name is Elvis Presley." I thought that's the weirdest name I've ever heard. Then they played "That's All Right, Mama". I'd never really heard anything like that before. "Mystery Train" is my favorite rock and roll record of all time. I don't know what it is about the song, there's just something about it that I love, from the title to the syncopation of the guitar lick.

**john fogerty:** The first record I heard by Elvis was "Blue Moon Of Kentucky" on KWBR, the R&B station out of Oakland. Elvis' Sun Records had a big effect on me. I think I was 10 when I first heard them. I was totally wild for Elvis and I was totally fascinated and drawn to that sound. Musically, he was the wildest.

In 1956 Elvis was James Dean but doing rock and roll. Elvis looked like what his music sounded like. A lot of the blues guys looked pretty sedate and were not wild and crazy. Elvis was shakin' and gyrating. When you see those old *Ed Sullivan* shows, it looks like he's coming out of his clothes practically. I remember I was in some kind of café and I heard "My Baby Left Me" for the first time. It turned out that it was the other side of "I Want You, I Need You, I Love You." (Sings like Elvis) "My baby left me…" I knew it was Elvis but I said, "What the heck is that?" Later I recorded it the best I could with Creedence (Clearwater Revival) but it still was a little smooth for my taste. Elvis' version was raw and just great and wonderful. After Elvis came out of the Army his music became smoother. It's great music but it was not rockin'. He was starting to record with the Nashville guys who were great but it wasn't Elvis, Scotty and Bill. I've since forgiven Elvis (laughs) and I've grown to like some of his '60s material. "Suspicious Minds" is truly great and "Burning Love" too. I was told later that when Felton Jarvis went in to record "Burning Love" with Elvis that they were trying to get a Creedence feel. I was getting my feel from Elvis and Sun Records. I think at some point Elvis liked what Creedence was doing and thought that they should get back to what they used to do.

**JOE PERRY** (Aerosmith): Elvis started it all and then the Beatles and the Stones followed what he started. Elvis broke down the race barrier in music and consequently in society. I think Elvis's music is great and he's a brilliant singer. He could sing anything. I'm fascinated by Elvis's whole story. I regret never being able to see him live.

**DON FELDER** (The Eagles): Elvis was the most influential musician in rock history. He set a new direction and sound for rock that musicians even today are following. His "young rebel" looks, gyrations and sound rocked the world and set millions off buying records and clinging to their radios to hear his new inspiring sound. Millions of people, including myself started playing guitar after seeing Elvis with hopes and dreams of becoming like him in some small way. His legacy, songs and influence still resonates throughout the world of music today and will echo in the future in the songs and music of those to follow. Elvis has NOT left the building!

**LINDSEY BUCKINGHAM** (Fleetwood Mac): I first became interested in rock and roll after hearing "Heartbreak Hotel" by Elvis Presley. I was only six-years old at the time and my brother brought home the single. The music was so powerful and I just loved it. It sparked the imagination of many of us. My brother was a great aficionado of early rock and roll and I was lucky to have someone old enough to be buying all those great Elvis 45's. I would spend hours in my brother's bedroom listening to all those early Elvis songs over and over. In fact, I learned how to play guitar listening to those Elvis records along with records by Chuck Berry and Fats Domino. Elvis synthesized elements of R&B and country and put it into a form that was acceptable for a broad white audience. He made it exciting and he was able to be the messenger of that music, which was still completely subversive but wasn't perceived as too subversive for the masses.

**DUSTY HILL** (ZZ Top): I watched the '68 special live as it was broadcast and loved it. That black leather suit was something but I was into the jumpsuit era Elvis. I saw him in the early days when I was a kid when he played the Texas State Fair and I've followed all aspects of his career. Later I saw him play at the Astrodome and I'd borrowed a pair of binoculars from Billy Gibbons' mom. When Elvis came on she almost jerked my head off grabbing them from around my neck! My wife's doll collection includes a leather suited Elvis and I had a jumpsuit-era telephone. Elvis is forever.

**RICHARD CARPENTER** (The Carpenters): I was a big fan of Elvis's '50s rockabilly stuff, the pre-Army music. Elvis wanted to be Perry Como, Bing Crosby, Frank Sinatra and Dean Martin. He wanted to be a balladeer and to me he was a born rocker and rockabilly artist. There was a freshness to his whole sound. He had a perfect feel. He grew up listening to country and rhythm and blues and when he combined those influences it really became something unique. I'm old enough to remember parents having a fit over Elvis. They thought that he was a threat and dangerous with songs like "Don't Be Cruel," "Teddy Bear" and "All Shook Up," but they were really lightweight stuff. But yet he was so different for Middle America that they considered him a threat. I'll never get tired of listening to those songs. There are certain records that you loved at one point in time and that were played so much that you don't care to hear them again. But with Elvis's '50s records, you could have heard them 100,000 times, but each time you hear it is like the first time. And the early Elvis stuff is that way with me.

**chris isaak:** Growing up my mom did all our shopping in the secondhand store and I still remember finding an old Elvis 45 in a stack of used records. It was "I'll Never Let You Go" on the Sun Sessions label. That record was my first taste. I didn't know at the time what the Sun Sessions were or that there were more songs from that time. I just knew it was my favorite record and I wore it out. Then I was on the boxing team years later in Japan and hap-

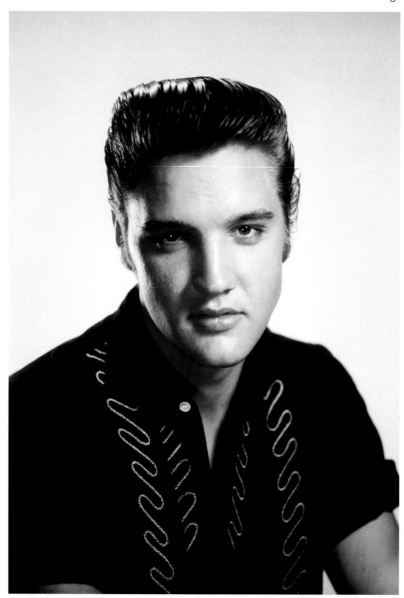

pened into a little record shop and found a Japanese release of "The Sun Sessions". I bought it and within a few weeks I was letting my regulation flattop grow out so I could slick it up in the front and look like the King. Skip ahead a few more years and I got to actually play with the Jorda- naires, DJ Fontana and Scotty Moore. I think I just about passed out to meet Scotty Moore and getting to have him play "Blue Moon" while I sang was one of those moments that you think, "I'm dreamin'...I'm gonna wake up any minute". And finally I was on the road with my band and I was reading an interview with Sam Phillips who produced all the Sun Sessions. At the end of the interview the writer asked Sam what new artists he was listening to or liked, and Sam said "Chris Isaak". I cried. I don't think any award I could ever win would mean as much to me, because it was Sam Phillips and Elvis and Scotty that made me pick up a guitar and just go for it. When I meet Elvis I'm gonna sure thank him for that.

**paul stanley** (KISS): My attraction to Elvis was the incredible animal magnetism and swagger that the guy had onstage in the early days. There was a danger about what he did that was really the essence of what rock and roll is at its best. It was dangerous and yet it was so entic- ing and appealing. The little girls didn't quite understand what they were squealing at but you'd see that smile on his face because he knew. He's a very underrated singer and a great song stylist. His talent was staggering. He was one of a kind.

**ace frehley** (KISS): The day Elvis died KISS was playing San Francisco's Cow Palace and I dedicated "Rock and Roll All Nite" to him. Simply put...he was "the King" and always will be!

**dave clark:** Elvis is in the same league as an actor like James Dean, who's still as big now as he ever was. Same goes for Marilyn Monroe. They're all legends that will just go on forever and Elvis is the ultimate icon in rock and roll.

**paul rodgers** (Bad Company): In the mid seventies I went to see Elvis at the Forum in L.A. My manager Peter Grant brought me an autograph with the message, "Take time to live, Elvis". He died a few years later. I didn't fully appreciate his words at the time but I believe it is a message for us all. Elvis's voice remains warm, wild and rebellious....always the King!

**jackie deshannon:** Elvis was very enlightened, he had spiritual depth. That's exactly what people connected with. He was an original, one of a kind, and you can't manufacture someone like that. I really believe that fame was something that came along with the package. It didn't faze him like some of the artists today who are so puffed up and enamored with who they are. Elvis never was. When he was traveling around doing these shows in the '50s Elvis was told, "Your fans just ripped up your new car" and he said, "Well, they bought 'em for me so they can do whatever they want." That's how he felt. Nothing made him happier that being onstage and performing for his fans. Performing was in his DNA.

**millie kirkham:** I'm proud that I sang with a guy that became a legend but the main thing is I'm proud of the fact that he was my friend. He was friends with all of the people that he worked with. When we recorded or performed together it was like a little family reunion. He could be plain old Elvis. He didn't have to be superstar Elvis when he was around us. We treated him like he was one of us and he enjoyed that because he didn't have a chance to do that very often.

**joe esposito:** I don't think Elvis ever realized the effect he had on people's lives. He sang from the heart and that's why people loved him so much. Knowing Elvis through the years, none of us realized the power this man had around the world.

**june juanico:** Twenty years ago, my daughter, Tori was living in Las Vegas and working at the Imperial Hotel. She was walking through the lobby of the Hilton Hotel, and there's a big statue of Elvis. My grandson, Dallas, who was three years old at the time, tugged at my daughter's shirttail and said, "Look mama, that's Elvis." My daughter couldn't wait to call me to tell me what Dallas said. It just blew me away that a three-year old child would know who Elvis was.

**paul simon:** Going to Graceland affected me in an interesting way. I went through the whole tour and I kept thinking it's so naïve, it's almost embarrassing. I wandered through the house thinking about all the decorations and all the awards. Then I came to the end where the graves were. It said something on Elvis's grave like "Elvis Aron Presley, whose music touched the hearts of people all over the world" and I started to cry. It's really true, this guy touched my life and touched people's hearts all over the world.

**The International Hotel, Las Vegas, Nevada**

**July 31, 1969** Opening Night

*Set list:* Blue Suede Shoes - I Got A Woman - That's All Right - All Shook Up - Jailhouse Rock / Don't Be Cruel - Heartbreak Hotel - Love Me Tender - Hound Dog - Memories - My Babe - I Can't Stop Loving You - In the Ghetto - Suspicious Minds - Yesterday / Hey Jude - Johnny B Goode - Mystery Train / Tiger Man - What'd I Say - Can't Help Falling in Love

**August 1, 1969** Dinner Show

*Set list:* Blue Suede Shoes - I Got A Woman - All Shook Up - Love Me Tender - Jailhouse Rock / Don't Be Cruel - Heartbreak Hotel - Hound Dog - Memories - Mystery Train / Tiger Man - Monologue about his life and career - Baby, What You Want Me To Do - Are You Lonesome Tonight - Yesterday / Hey Jude - Introductions - In the Ghetto - Suspicious Minds - Can't Help Falling in Love

**August 3, 1969** Dinner Show, Soundboard recording

*Set list:* Blue Suede Shoes - I Got A Woman – Polk Salad Annie (1 line) - All Shook Up - Love Me Tender - Jailhouse Rock / Don't Be Cruel - Heartbreak Hotel - Hound Dog - Memories - Mystery Train / Tiger Man - Monologue about his life and career - Blue Hawaii (Part) - Baby, What You Want Me To Do (+) - Are You Lonesome Tonight – Yesterday / Hey Jude - Introductions - In the Ghetto - Suspicious Minds - What'd I Say (*) - Can't Help Falling in Love (*)

*Released on:*
Complete Show - CD Opening Night
(Fort Baxter A.S CD 731-69)

Complete Show - CD Elvis Meets The Beatles
(Teddy Bear TB 69)

Complete Show - CD Elvis Live-Unlicensed (SW 115).

Complete Show - CD A Hot Night in Vegas (Delta Blues)

(*) - Here I Go Again (DAE 3595-5)

(+) - Thank You Very Much (Fort Baxter 2304)

*Note: "What'd I Say" and "Can't Help Falling in Love" were released on the bootleg CD Here I Go Again (DAE 3595-5) to make that release look like a complete show.*

**August 4, 1969** Dinner and Midnight Show

*Set list:* Blue Suede Shoes - I Got a Woman -Love Me Tender -Heartbreak Hotel - All Shook Up -Don't Be Cruel-Are You Lonesome Tonight-Jailhouse Rock- Hound Dog- In the Ghetto - Tiger Man- What'd I Say -Baby, What You Want Me To Do –Yesterday - Can't Help Falling in Love

*No complete track listing exists*

**August 5, 1969** Midnight Show

*Audience recording*

*Set list:* Blue Suede Shoes (Elvis starts at the wrong place during the intro) - I Got A Woman - All Shook Up (intro only) - All Shook Up - Polk Salad Annie (1 line) - Love Me Tender - Jailhouse Rock / Don't Be Cruel - Heartbreak Hotel - Hound Dog – Memories - Mystery Train / Tiger Man - Monologue about his life and career - Farther Along (one line) - Baby, What You Want Me To Do – Runaway - Are You Lonesome Tonight – Yesterday / Hey Jude – Band Introductions - Introduces Darlene Love and Bill Medley - In the Ghetto - Suspicious Minds - What'd I Say - Can't Help Falling in Love

*Available as a CD-R only release*

**August 6, 1969** Dinner Show

*Audience recording*

*Set list:* Blue Suede Shoes - I Got A Woman - All Shook Up - Love Me Tender - Jailhouse Rock / Don't Be Cruel - Heartbreak Hotel - Hound Dog - Memories - Mystery Train / Tiger Man - Viva Las Vegas (just the first word as a request for a fan) - Blue Hawaii (1 line) - Monologue about his life and career - Baby, What You Want Me To Do - Runaway - Are You Lonesome Tonight (incomplete, beginning is missing) – Yesterday / Hey Jude (part missing between both songs) - Introductions - In the Ghetto - Suspicious Minds - What'd I Say - Can't Help Falling in Love

*Released on:*
CD The Return of the Tiger Man (Tiger 1000)

**August 7, 1969** Dinner and Midnight Show

Set list: Blue Suede Shoes - I Got A Woman - All Shook Up - Love Me Tender - Jailhouse Rock / Don't Be Cruel - Heartbreak Hotel - Hound Dog - Memories - Mystery Train / Tiger Man - Baby, What You Want Me To Do - Monologue about his life and career - Runaway - Are You Lonesome Tonight - Yesterday / Hey Jude - Introductions - In the Ghetto - Suspicious Minds - What I'd Say - Can't Help Falling in Love

*Same track list at both shows*

**August 12, 1969** Dinner Show

*Audience recording*

*Set list:* Blue Suede Shoes - I Got A Woman - All Shook Up - Love Me Tender - Jailhouse Rock / Don't Be Cruel - Heartbreak Hotel - Hound Dog - Instrumental part by James Burton - Memories - Mystery Train / Tiger Man - Monologue about his life and career - Hound Dog (1 line) - Baby, What You Want Me To Do - Runaway - Are You Lonesome Tonight - Yesterday / Hey Jude - Introductions - In the Ghetto - Suspicious Minds - What'd I Say - Can't Help Falling in Love

*Available as a CD-R only release*

**August 12, 1969** Midnight Show

*Set list:* Blue Suede Shoes - I Got A Woman - All Shook Up - Dialogue - Love Me Tender - Jailhouse Rock / Don't Be Cruel - Heartbreak Hotel - Hound Dog - Instrumental - Memories - Dialogue - Mystery Train / Tiger Man - Monologue about his life and career - Baby, What You Want Me To Do - Runaway - Are You Lonesome Tonight -Yesterday / Hey Jude - Introductions - In the Ghetto - Suspicious Minds - What'd I Say - Can't Help Falling in Love

**August 13, 1969** Dinner Show

*Audience recording*

*Set list:* Blue Suede Shoes - I Got A Woman - All Shook Up - Love Me Tender - Jailhouse Rock / Don't Be Cruel - Heartbreak Hotel- Hound Dog - Memories - Mystery Train / Tiger Man - Monologue about his life and career – Baby, What You Want Me To Do - Runaway - Are You Lonesome Tonight - Yesterday / Hey Jude - Introductions - In the Ghetto (incomplete, only beginning and ending on CDR) - Suspicious Minds - What'd I Say (no dialogue after What'd I Say, just a tape cut and straight into the opening bars of Can't Help Falling in Love - incomplete)

*Available as a CD-R only release*

*Note: There are a lot of small tape cuts between the songs.*

**August 14, 1969** Dinner Show

*Audience recording*

*Set list:* Blue Suede Shoes - I Got A Woman - All Shook Up - Viva Las Vegas (1 line) - Love Me Tender - Jailhouse Rock / Don't Be Cruel - Heartbreak Hotel - Elvis Talks - Hound Dog - Memories - Mystery Train / Tiger Man - Monologue about his life and career - Baby, What You Want Me To Do - Surrender (1 line) - Runaway - Are You Lonesome Tonight – Yesterday / Hey Jude - Introductions - In the Ghetto - Suspicious Minds - What'd I Say - Can't Help Falling in Love

*Released on*: LP Back in Vegas

CD Vegas Memories (PCD 690812)

CD The Winner Back in Vegas (no label)

*Note: Both CD's contain an incomplete show. On both CD's "Love Me Tender" is missing and "Blue Suede Shoes" and "Are You Lonesome Tonight" are added from RCA's Elvis In Person album, although both songs do not originate from this date. Both CD's also mention August 12th as the recording date, which is incorrect. The CD-R version contains the complete show and is correctly dated.*

*Available as a CD-R only release*

**August 15, 1969** Dinner or Midnight Show?

*Audience recording*

*Set list:* Blue Suede Shoes - I Got A Woman - All Shook Up - Love Me Tender - Jailhouse Rock / Don't Be Cruel - Heartbreak Hotel - Hound Dog - Memories - Mystery Train / Tiger Man - Monologue about his life and career - Baby, What You Want Me To Do - Runaway - Are You Lonesome Tonight – Yesterday / Hey Jude - Introductions - Introduction Jerry Lee Lewis - Whole Lotta Shakin' Goin' On (1 line) - In the Ghetto - Suspicious Minds - What'd I Say - Can't Help Falling in Love (incomplete)

*Available as a CD-R only release*

**August 16, 1969** Midnight Show

*Audience recording*

*Set list:* Blue Suede Shoes - I Got A Woman - All Shook Up - Love Me Tender (incomplete, beginning is missing) - My Babe - Such A Night (1 line) - Jailhouse Rock / Don't Be Cruel - Heartbreak Hotel - Hound Dog - Memories - Mystery Train / Tiger Man - Monologue about his life and career (incomplete) - Baby, What You Want Me To Do – Runaway (incomplete, ending is missing) - Are You Lonesome Tonight - Yesterday / Hey Jude – Introductions - Introduction Harry James - In the Ghetto - Suspicious Minds - What'd I Say - Can't Help Falling in Love

*Available as a CD-R only release*

*Wrongly dated as August 16, 1969 Dinner Show*

**August 18, 1969** Dinner Show

*Audience recording*

*Set list:* Blue Suede Shoes - I Got A Woman - All Shook Up - Love Me Tender - Jailhouse Rock / Don't Be Cruel - Heartbreak Hotel - Hound Dog - Memories (incomplete) - Mystery Train / Tiger Man - Monologue about his life and career (incomplete) - Baby, What You Want Me To Do (incomplete, intro only) - Runaway - Funny How Time Slips Away (incomplete, beginning is missing) - Are You Lonesome Tonight (incomplete, beginning is missing) - Yesterday (incomplete, beginning is missing) / Hey Jude (incomplete, largest part is missing) - In the Ghetto (incomplete, intro only) – Suspicious Minds

*Note: This recording contains an incomplete show. The introductions and the complete versions of "What'd I Say" and "Can't Help Falling in Love" are missing. In addition, there are many tape cuts between the songs and many songs are incomplete.*

*Available as a CD-R only release*

**August 19, 1969** Midnight Show

*Set list:* Blue Suede Shoes - I Got A Woman - All Shook Up - Love Me Tender - My Babe - Jailhouse Rock / Don't Be Cruel - Heartbreak Hotel - Hound Dog - Memories - Mystery Train / Tiger Man - Monologue about his life and career – Baby, What You Want Me To Do - Runaway - Are You Lonesome Tonight - Yesterday / Hey Jude - Introductions - In the Ghetto - Suspicious Minds - What'd I Say - Can't Help Falling in Love

**August 20, 1969** Dinner Show

*Set list:* Blue Suede Shoes - I Got A Woman - All Shook Up - Love Me Tender - Jailhouse Rock / Don't Be Cruel - Heartbreak Hotel - Hound Dog - Mystery Train / Tiger Man - Monologue about his life and career – Baby, What You Want Me To Do - Are You Lonesome Tonight – It's Now Or Never (part) – Yesterday / Hey Jude - In the Ghetto - Suspicious Minds – Can't Help Falling in Love

**August 21, 1969** Dinner Show

*RCA recording*

*Set list:* Blue Suede Shoes - I Got A Woman - All Shook Up - Love Me Tender - My Babe - Jailhouse Rock / Don't Be Cruel - Heartbreak Hotel - Hound Dog - Memories - Mystery Train / Tiger Man - Monologue about his life and career - Baby, What You Want Me To Do - Runaway - Are You Lonesome Tonight – Words - Yesterday / Hey Jude - Introductions - In the Ghetto - Suspicious Minds - What'd I Say - Can't Help Falling in Love

*Note: This show was used by RCA to test the sound in anticipation of officially recording the Midnight show. Only parts of "Yesterday / Hey Jude," "In the Ghetto" and "Suspicious Minds" were recorded.*

**August 21, 1969** Midnight Show

*RCA recording*

*Set list:* Blue Suede Shoes - I Got A Woman - All Shook Up - Love Me Tender - My Babe - Jailhouse Rock / Don't Be Cruel - Heartbreak Hotel - Hound Dog - I Can't Stop Loving You - My Babe - Mystery Train / Tiger Man - Monologue about his life and career (*) - Funny How Time Slips Away (1 line) - Baby, What You Want Me To Do - Surrender (part) (+) - Runaway - Are You Lonesome Tonight - Words - Yesterday / Hey Jude (*) - Introductions (*) (+) - Happy Birthday to James Burton (*)(+) - In the Ghetto (*) - Suspicious Minds (*) - What'd I Say (*) - Can't Help Falling in Love (*)

*Released on:*
Complete Show - CD Viva Las Vegas (Sony / BMG)

(*) - CD/LP The Legend Lives On (Presley Collection Series PCS 1001)

(+) - CD/LP Box Collector's Gold (BMG)

*Notes: The start of "Blue Suede Shoes" was not recorded by RCA; the beginning of "Blue Suede Shoes" on Viva Las Vegas was culled from the August 22nd Dinner Show and spliced in to make it seem complete. The "Monologue" as recorded by RCA is incomplete (tape cut in middle and tape damage at the end); on Viva Las Vegas the "Monologue" from the August 22nd Dinner Show and spliced in to make it seem complete. The start of "Baby, What You Want Me To Do" has tape damage; on Viva Las Vegas the beginning of "Baby, What You Want Me To Do" from the August 22nd Dinner show was spliced in to make it seem complete. Part of the original "Monologue" from this show can only be found on the bootleg The Legend Lives On. The introductions were shortened when released on Collector's Gold.*

**August 22, 1969** Dinner Show

*RCA recording*

*Set list:* Blue Suede Shoes - I Got A Woman - All Shook Up - Love Me Tender - Jailhouse Rock / Don't Be Cruel - Heartbreak Hotel - Hound Dog - Memories - Mystery Train / Tiger Man - Monologue about his life and career (*) - Baby, What You Want Me To Do - Runaway – Funny How Time Slips Away - Are You Lonesome Tonight - Yesterday / Hey Jude - Introductions - In the Ghetto - Suspicious Minds (+) - What'd I Say - Can't Help Falling in Love

*Released on:*
Complete Show - CD Elvis in Person - Expanded (Follow That Dream Records)

(*) - CD Viva Las Vegas (Sony/BMG)

(+) - CD/LP Box Behind Closed Doors (Audifon) and A Dinner Date with Elvis (Live Archives 1021).

*Notes: During the "Monologue" Elvis mentions that Mrs. Tippler is in the audience, and that it's her birthday. She was the wife of Elvis's first employer, Crown Electric. A spliced version of "Suspicious Minds" from this show spliced at 2:00 with "Uuuhhh, uhhhhh, Yeah, yeah" onwards from an as yet unknown performance of the song (wrongly dated as being from February 16, 1970) can be found on the bootleg box set Behind Closed Doors and the CD reissue of A Dinner Date With Elvis.*

**August 22, 1969** Midnight Show

*RCA recording*

*Set list:* Blue Suede Shoes - I Got A Woman (*) - All Shook Up - Love Me Tender (**) - Jailhouse Rock / Don't Be Cruel (**)(+) - Heartbreak Hotel - Hound Dog - My Babe (++) - Mystery Train / Tiger Man (**) - Monologue About His Life And Career - Baby, What You Want Me To Do (++) - Runaway (++) – Funny How Time Slips Away (++) - Are You Lonesome Tonight - Yesterday / Hey Jude - Introductions - In the Ghetto - Suspicious Minds - What'd I Say (++) - Can't Help Falling in Love

*Released on:*
(*) - CD Good Times Never Seemed So Good (Capt. Marvel Jnr), CD/LP Box Behind Closed Doors Audifon) and A Dinner Date with Elvis (Live Archives 1021)

(**) - CD/LP Box Collector's Gold (BMG)

(+) - CD Live Greatest Hits (BMG)

(++) - CD Box Today Tomorrow & Forever (BMG)

**August 23, 1969** Dinner Show

*RCA recording*

*Set list:* Blue Suede Shoes - I Got A Woman - All Shook Up - Love Me Tender - Jailhouse Rock / Don't Be Cruel - Heartbreak Hotel - Hound Dog - I Can't Stop Loving You - My Babe - Mystery Train / Tiger Man - Monologue about his life and career - Baby, What You Want Me To Do - Runaway - Are You Lonesome Tonight - Yesterday / Hey Jude - Introductions - In the Ghetto - Suspicious Minds - What'd I Say (**) - Can't Help Falling in Love

**August 23, 1969** Midnight Show

*RCA recording*

*Set list:* Blue Suede Shoes - I Got A Woman - All Shook Up - Elvis welcomes the audience - Love Me Tender - Jailhouse Rock / Don't Be Cruel - Heartbreak Hotel - Hound Dog - Memories - Mystery Train / Tiger Man - Monologue about his life and career - Baby, What You Want Me To Do - Runaway (*) - Loving You (part) (**) (***) - Reconsider Baby(**) (***) - Are You Lonesome Tonight - Yesterday / Hey Jude - Introductions - In the Ghetto - Suspicious Minds - What'd I Say (**) (+) - Can't Help Falling in Love

*Released on:*
Complete - CD Elvis at the International (Follow That Dream Records)

(*) – Elvis On Stage (BMG 1999 Edition)

(**) - CD/LP Box Collector's Gold (BMG)

(***) - CD Elvis In Person - Expanded (Follow That Dream Records)

(+) - Greatest Hits Volume 1 (RCA) /The Sound Of Your Cry (RCA - UK only)

*Notes: An edited version of "'What'd I Say" was first released on Greatest Hits Volume 1 and the UK LP The Sound Of Your Cry, and then later on the bootleg Old Ones New Ones & In Between (Groti GR105). The unedited version was first released on BMG's Collector's Gold, and later on the bootleg Philadelphia '77 where it was wrongly dated as being from 1973.*

## August 24, 1969 Dinner Show

*RCA recording*

*Set list*: Blue Suede Shoes - I Got A Woman - All Shook Up - Elvis Welcomes the audience - Love Me Tender - Jailhouse Rock / Don't Be Cruel - Heartbreak Hotel (**)(+) - Hound Dog - I Can't Stop Loving You - Johnny B Goode - Monologue about his life and career - Baby, What You Want Me To Do - Runaway - Elvis introduces the Colonel's wife, Marie who is in the audience after having an operation - Are You Lonesome Tonight - Yesterday (*) / Hey Jude - Introductions - Elvis introduces George Hamilton - In the Ghetto - Suspicious Minds - What'd I Say - Can't Help Falling in Love

*Released on:*

Complete - CD Box Elvis Live in Las Vegas (BMG)

(*) - CD/LP Box Elvis Aron Presley (BMG)

(**) - CD/LP Box Collector's Gold (BMG)

(+) - CD Live Greatest Hits (BMG)

*Notes: BMG did this show a disservice by placing the "Monologue" about his life at the end of the show.*

*The as yet still unreleased 1969 Master of "Jailhouse Rock / Don't Be Cruel" (XPA5 2317) is spliced from "Don't Be Cruel" recorded at this show and "Jailhouse Rock" culled from the August 26th Dinner Show.*

## August 24, 1969 Midnight Show

*RCA recording*

Set list: Blue Suede Shoes (***) - I Got A Woman (***) - All Shook Up (***) - Elvis welcomes the audience (***) - Love Me Tender (***) - Jailhouse Rock / Don't Be Cruel (***) - Heartbreak Hotel (***) - Hound Dog (***) - I Can't Stop Loving You - Johnny B Goode (*) (**) - Monologue about his life and career - Baby, What You Want Me To Do (**) - Runaway - Are You Lonesome Tonight (*) (+) - Words (**) - Yesterday / Hey Jude (***) - Introductions - In the Ghetto - Suspicious Minds (***) - What'd I Say - Can't Help Falling in Love (***)

*Released on:*

(In) Complete - CD Here I Go Again (DAE 3595-5) wrongly dated as August 23rd 1969 Dinner Show

(*) - CD/LP Elvis In Person (BMG/RCA)

(**) - CD Box Platinum – A Life in Music (BMG)

(***) - CD/Book Writing For The King (Follow That Dream Records)

(+) - CD Live Greatest Hits (BMG)

*Notes: Most of this show (from "Blue Suede Shoes" to "In The Ghetto") can be found on the bootleg Here I Go Again (DAE 3595-5) but is wrongly dated as being recorded at the August 23rd 1969 Dinner Show. "Johnny B Goode" was issued a new matrix number (WPA5 2595) when released on the Platinum box set by mistake. "Yesterday / Hey Jude" on Writing For The King is wrongly dated as being from August 25th Dinner Show. "Are You Lonesome Tonight" can also be found on the bootlegs Winner Back in Vegas and Vegas Memories. "In the Ghetto" on the Elvis Aron Presley box set is listed as being from this date, but that date is incorrect.*

## August 25, 1969 Dinner Show

*RCA recording*

*Set list:* Blue Suede Shoes (*) (+) - I Got A Woman (*) - All Shook Up - Love Me Tender - Jailhouse Rock / Don't Be Cruel - Heartbreak Hotel - Hound Dog - Memories (*) - Mystery Train / Tiger Man - Monologue about his life and career - Baby, What You Want Me To Do - Runaway (++)(+++) - Funny How Time Slips Away (*) - Are You Lonesome Tonight - Words (***) - Yesterday (++) (+++) / Hey Jude - Introductions - In the Ghetto (**) - Suspicious Minds - What'd I Say - Can't Help Falling in Love

*Released on:*

(*) - CD/LP Box Collector's Gold (BMG)

(**) - CD/LP Elvis In Person (BMG/RCA)

(***) - CD/Book Writing For The King
(Follow That Dream Records)

(+) - CD Live Greatest Hits (BMG)

(++) - CD/LP On Stage 1970 (BMG/RCA)

(+++) - CD Good Times Never Seemed So Good (Capt. Marvel Jnr) - Undubbed

*Notes: "Funny How Time Slips Away" was issued a new matrix number (WPA5 2518) when released on the Platinum box set. The complete "Yesterday / Hey Jude" was released on the 1999 upgrade of On Stage 1970. The undubbed version of "Yesterday" (without "Hey Jude") can also be found on the bootleg The Legend Lives On (Presley Collection Series PCS 1001).*

## August 25, 1969 Midnight Show

*RCA recording*

*Set list:* Blue Suede Shoes (*) - I Got A Woman - All Shook Up (*) - Love Me Tender - Jailhouse Rock / Don't Be Cruel - Heartbreak Hotel - Hound Dog (*) - I Can't Stop Loving You (*) - My Babe (*) - Mystery Train / Tiger Man (*) - Monologue about his life and career - Baby, What You Want Me To Do - Runaway - Are You Lonesome Tonight - Words (*) - Yesterday / Hey Jude - Introductions - Introductions Nancy Sinatra, Mac Davis, Buddy Haggard, Tom Jones, Shelley Fabares - It's Now Or Never (1 line) - In the Ghetto (+) - Suspicious Minds - What'd I Say - Polk Salad Annie (1 line) - Can't Help Falling in Love

Released On:
(*) - CD/LP Elvis In Person (BMG/RCA)

(+) - CD/Book Writing For The King (Follow That Dream Records)

*Available as a CD-R only release - audience recording*

*Notes: The dialogue before "Hound Dog" on the Elvis In Person CD is completely different from the dialogue before the song on the CD-R with the complete audience recorded show. Perhaps BMG removed the dialogue from another show because of the rough language? The dialogue between 'Hound Dog" and the following song, "I Can't Stop Loving You," is also completely different but the songs are the same. The dialogue before "My Babe" comes from another show, as it can be heard before a version of "Baby, What You Want Me To Do" on one of RCA's releases. On the audience tape, Elvis goes straight into "My Babe" after he ended "I Can't Stop Loving You." The dialogue between "My Babe" and "Mystery Train/Tiger Man" has been edited also on Elvis In Person, again because of the rough language. ".Are You Lonesome Tonight" can also be found on the bootlegs Winner Back in Vegas and Vegas Memories.*

## August 26, 1969 Dinner Show

*RCA recording*

*Set list:* Blue Suede Shoes - I Got A Woman - All Shook Up - Love Me Tender - Jailhouse Rock / Don't Be Cruel - Heartbreak Hotel - Hound Dog - Inherit the Wind (+) - My Babe (**) - Monologue about his life and career - Baby, What You Want Me To Do - Runaway - Are You Lonesome Tonight - Words - Yesterday / Hey Jude - Introductions - In the Ghetto - Suspicious Minds (*) - What'd I Say - Can't Help Falling in Love (*)

*Released on:*
(*) - CD/LP Elvis In Person (BMG/RCA)

(**) - CD/LP Box Elvis Aron Presley (BMG)

(+) - CD/LP Box Collector's Gold (BMG) and Elvis In Person - Expanded (Follow That Dream Records)

*Notes: "Inherit the Wind" was issued a new matrix number (WPA5 2527) when released on the Collector's Gold set.*

*The as yet still unreleased 1969 Master of "Jailhouse Rock / Don't Be Cruel" (XPA5 2317) is spliced from "Jailhouse Rock" recorded from this show and "Don't Be Cruel" from the August 24th Dinner Show. "My Babe" can also be found on the bootleg "Old Ones New Ones & In Between (Groti GR105). "Inherit the Wind" can also be found on the bootleg "Inherit the Wind" (Tiger 4000).*

## August 26, 1969 Midnight Show

*RCA recording*

*Set list:* Blue Suede Shoes - I Got A Woman - All Shook Up - Love Me Tender - Jailhouse Rock / Don't Be Cruel - Heartbreak Hotel - Hound Dog - I Can't Stop Loving You - Mystery Train / Tiger Man - Monologue about his Life and Career - Baby, What You Want Me To Do (**) – Runaway (**) - Introduction Del Shannon - Are You Lonesome Tonight (Laughing Version) (*)(**) - Rubberneckin' (**) (with false start) (***) - Yesterday / Hey Jude - Introductions - This is the Story (**)(***) - In the Ghetto - Suspicious Minds - Can't Help Falling in Love

*Released On:*
Complete - All Shook Up (Follow That Dream Records)

(*) - CD/LP Box Elvis Aron Presley (BMG)

(**) - CD/LP Box Collector's Gold (BMG)

(***) - Elvis In Person - Expanded (Follow That Dream)

*Notes: "Rubberneckin'" (without false start) was issued a new matrix number (WPA5 2525) along with "This is the Story" (WPA5 2526) when released on the Collector's Gold box set. The laughing version of "Are You Lonesome Tonight" was also issued as a single in the UK in 1982.*

*Available as a CD-R only release - audience recording*

*Note: This audience recording is spliced from different shows*

## August 27, 1969 Dinner Show

*Audience recording*

Songs performed at this show:

Its Now Or Never (1 verse) - Loving You (1 verse) - One Night - Love Me – Baby, What You Want Me To Do - Runaway

Track listing incomplete

## August 27, 1969 Midnight Show

*Audience recording*

Songs performed at this show:

Baby, What You Want Me To Do - Johnny B. Goode

Track listing incomplete

*Note: No set list information is known about the following shows nor do any official or unofficial recordings exist:*

8-1-69 (DS & MS)
8-2-69 (DS & MS)
8-3-69 (MS)
8-5-69 (DS)
8-6-69 (MS)
8-8-69 (DS & MS)
8-9-69 (DS & MS)
8-10-69 (DS & MS)
8-11-69 (DS & MS)
8-13-69 (MS)
8-14-69 (MS)
8-16-69 (DS)
8-17-69 (DS & MS)
8-18-69 (MS)
8-19-69 (DS)
8-20-69 (MS)
8-28-69 (DS & MS)

DS=dinner show
MS=midnight show

Additional thanks to David Wilson for his help.

(Author's note: all attempts were made to provide exact dates for the '69 live photos, however, many of the images provided by photographers and photo agencies were not dated hence the impossible task of assigning a specific date).

# acknowledgments

**Special thanks** to Bill Bram (www.elvisframebyframe.com) and Ernst Jorgensen for their friendship, support and belief in the project.

**A hearty round of applause** for Joan and Paul Gansky who graciously made available various '68 Comeback special and International Hotel material culled from their treasure chest of Elvis memorabilia.

**A thunderous cheer** to Robert Dye and Scott Williams of Elvis Presley Enterprises for their support and enthusiasm about the project.

**All access backstage privileges** to Andrew Hearn (www.essentialelvis.com) and Russ Howe (www.kingcandids.com) for their constant words of encouragement and expertise.

**My gratitude** to Peter Verbruggen of Elvis Matters for being an early believer in the project and for his continued support (www.elvismatters.com).

**Thanks** to Joseph Kereta (www.elvisnow.com) for providing an array of International Hotel ephemera and Bob Klein (www.tcbpotos.net) for his gracious use of various images.

**A standing ovation:** Margie Adamsky, Samantha Adamsky, Tim Adamsky, Denny Anderson, Piers Beagley/ Elvis Information Network (www.elvisinfonet.com), Mitch Blank, John Bionelli, Steve Binder, Jim Bullotta, Shantel Burgess/Retna, Maria Columbus, Ray Connolly, Mac Davis, Hank deLespinasse, Andrew DeYoung, Rosa DiSalvo/Getty Images, Paul Dowling (www.worldwideelvis.com), Andy Dumas, Dave Dunton, Larry Elliot, Keith Flynn, Jay Gilbert, Jean-Marc Gargiulo, Mike Giesbrecht, Bud Glass, Margo Grace, Gloria Greer, Ross Halfin, Louis Hirshorn, Jeremy Holiday, Mark James, Jay S. Jacobs, Lisa Jacob/Las Vegas News Bureau, Glen Johnson, Susan Katila, Carol Kaye, Elliot Kendall, Roger Kjøhl, Harvey Kubernik, Ron Landheer, Andylon Lensen, Daniel Lombardy, Bob Merlis, Ann Moses, Julie Mundy, Megan Murphy/Elvis Unlimited (www.elvisunlimited.com), Loanne Parker, Pep/For Elvis CD Collectors, Joe Perry, Jim Pierson, Helmut Radermacher, Mike Rinaldi, Don and Irene Robertson, Cynthia Kereluk Rodgers, Paul Rodgers, Jerry Schilling, David Schwartz/UNLV, Carol Sharp, Carol Paula Sharp, Jim Sharp, Paul Stanley, Ira Sternberg/Las Vegas Hilton, Jeff Suhs, Ian Fraser-Thomson, Lou Toomin, David Troedson/Elvis Australia (www.elvis.com.au/), Mike Weatherford, Mary Beth Whelan/Globe Photos, Fred Whobrey, David Wilson, Meghan Wright/Corbis, and My Favorite Pooches, Herman, Buddy and Cha-Cha.

Carrie would like to thank the Krugiltons, Michael and August, for their love and support.

In locating photographs taken 40 years ago, every effort has been made to track down the original copyright holders. However, for some of the images that has proved impossible. If your image was used in the book without proper credit, please contact the publisher.

All interviews for the book conducted by Ken Sharp unless otherwise noted.